MUSi W9-AMA-564 295

10⁹⁵

NETWORKING
IN THE
MUSIC
BUSINESS

DAN KIMPEL

Cincinnati, Ohio

ABOUT THE AUTHOR

In his long career in the music business, Dan Kimpel has been a songwriter, performer, producer, publicist and manager. He currently operates an artist management firm in Los Angeles and is advertising director for the Los Angeles Songwriters Showcase, an organization dedicated to serving and educating songwriters.

Networking in the Music Business. Copyright © 1993 by Dan Kimpel. Printed and bound in the United States of America. All rights reserved. No part of this book may be reproduced in any form or by any electronic or mechanical means including information storage and retrieval systems without permission in writing from the publisher, except by a reviewer, who may quote brief passages in a review. Published by Writer's Digest Books, an imprint of F&W Publications, Inc., 1507 Dana Avenue, Cincinnati, Ohio 45207. 1-800-289-0963. First edition.

This hardcover edition of *Networking in the Music Business* features a "self-jacket" that eliminates the need for a separate dust jacket. It provides sturdy protection for your book while it saves paper, trees and energy.

97   96   95   94   93   5   4   3   2   1

Library of Congress Cataloging-in-Publication Data

Kimple, Dan
    Networking in the music business / by Dan Kimpel. — 1st ed.
         p.   cm.
    Includes index.
    ISBN 0-89879-597-4 (hardcover)
    1. Musicians — Social networks. 2. Music trade — United States. I. Title.
ML3790.K46   1993
780'.23'73 — dc20   93-1814
                                                                          CIP
                                                                          MN

Edited by Mark Garvey
Designed by Paul Neff

Power Shmoozing, written by Terri Mandell, is published by First House Press, © 1992. Portions of *Power Shmoozing* are reprinted with the permission of the publisher.

ACKNOWLEDGMENTS

Thanks to my fellow Buckeye, Mark Garvey, for asking me to author this book and for his confidence, support and Post-it notes of suggestions throughout the process.

Mahalo nui to my client, collaborator and friend Keo for creating music that convinced me to begin my career in artist management. Thanks to my fellow authors and wonderful friends Jeffrey Tennyson and Marta Woodhull for proving to me that writing books could actually be done by human beings.

Thanks —

To all the global musicians whose conviction has given me their power: from Jamaica to New Orleans, the Ivory Coast to Sado Island, Japan, from Honolulu to Madagascar, from Tin Pan Alley to 16th Avenue South, from Senegal to the Sunset Strip.

To Donald Passman and all the professionals who shared their insight in these chapters, and for my long time Eagle Rock musical cohort, Tim Horrigan, for keeping the rock alive.

To all the staff of the Los Angeles Songwriters Showcase, past and present, who have helped so many songwriters the last twenty-odd years, especially LASS co-founders John Braheny and Len Chandler as well as Angela Taylor, Angelo Roman, Mandi-Martin Fox, Nan Surprenant and Josh Bernard.

To my family back in Lima, Ohio: my parents Rocky and Jo Ann Kimpel; my brother and sister-in-law, Dr. Jeff and Louise Kimpel; and my late Grandmother Ruth McClain and Aunt Dorothy McClain Councilman — thanks to all of you for your unwavering support lo these many years.

For Yuji Nishimoto: I never could have done any of this without your help. Thank you.

FOREWORD

This book is intended as a guide for the professional and the aspirant in all levels of the music industry. It represents the expert opinion of the author but may not be applicable in all situations. The networking resource guide at the end of the book is current at the time of this writing, but because of the nature of musicians and organizations, some of this information may have changed.

Each reader will hopefully apply any material in this book to his or her own circumstances but consult with legal and other appropriate professionals for advice as needed.

TABLE OF CONTENTS

If I woke up tomorrow, decided that my life's ambition was to design sports cars, then picked up the phone to convey this desire to the president of Toyota, I would most assuredly be brushed off as a lunatic. Sports cars are designed by people who have spent many years in design facilities and apprenticeships learning their craft; an outsider couldn't possibly with one phone call break into such an insular occupation or hope to achieve anything beyond the inevitable brush-off from an icy receptionist and a subsequent hang-up.

In the music business, on a daily basis, the telephone lines are clogged by callers certain that they are, or have, the "next big thing." Unwanted cartons of unlistened-to cassette tapes are unceremoniously deposited in trash receptacles while the myth of the pot of gold at the end of the rainbow continues to hypnotize yet another generation of performers and songwriters. Unscrupulous companies prey upon the unwary and uninformed, but the rainbow is an illusion, the gold is painted on, and only the con artists profit from the unrealistic dreams of stardom and success.

As the advertising director for the Los Angeles Songwriters Showcase, I have been in a position for the last five years to observe the thousands of people who desperately try to break into the music game. As a twenty-year veteran of the music industry, I've been in a key position to observe firsthand songwriters and performers who have broken through and sold millions of records. The latter possessed the necessary skills, but they also directed their own success through perseverance, people skills and, above all, an uncanny sense of networking.

Success in the music business is dependent on three key factors: who you know, what you know, and who knows you. Like any other business it's a chessboard of players, hustlers, wanna-be's, used-to-be's and someday-will-be's. In order to operate in this business, it is imperative that you understand who the key players are and what they do.

Almost no reputable record company will listen to an aspirant's tape unless it comes to them from a legitimate source with which they're familiar, and preferably have done business with in the past. Believe me, even with these limitations on their accessibility they're still overloaded, yet new songwriters, artists and performers are signed every year. How do they break through?

If you want national recognition you have to create a buzz in New York, Nashville or Los Angeles. If you want to stay on your home turf, you will have to play the same kind of game. Like other businesses, the music business has a healthy respect for initiative, and a quality commonly referred to as "chutzpah." This business, descended from rough and tumble 1950s New York, is not a place for the reticent or the timid. It possesses a very specific sense of finesse, though, and a constant agenda of personal contacts and paybacks.

WHAT IS NETWORKING?

In the broadest sense, networking refers to any alliance, relationship or communication with others in your field. This could be as simple as discussing with another musician what brand of guitar strings he uses when you encounter him at your local music store. When he invites you to his gig, or you invite him to yours, that's another step. When he refers you for a gig he can't work because of a prior commitment is when the network begins to work on an economic level. Suppose your imaginary friend's band signs with a major manager, publisher or record label. If your friend believes in your abilities, he is now in a key position to help you.

There is nothing new about networking; it's simply a new title given to an ancient methodology. In the music business though, there has never been a book to tell you how it works, give you tricks of the trade, and show you how to increase your odds with specific plans and methods.

Networking in the Music Business is a blueprint for success as well as an explanation of how things really happen, and why.

TWO TRUTHS

1. **Every networking trick in the book won't help you if you don't have the goods.** The information included here can help you to open up the doors, but once those doors are open you've got to have something amazing to shove inside. People who succeed as songwriters, performers, musicians and technical and support staff are incredibly good. In Los Angeles on any given night of the week you can attend an "industry showcase" and hear unsigned acts and talent who are far and away superior to the top-charting artists of the day.

But are they as original as those artists, as visionary, as inspired? If you are a songwriter, your songs have to be better than what you hear on the radio, not just as good, because those songs have already been proven, recorded, and most important, are making money for the writers and publishers.

Networking in the Music Business will not help you write songs, play, sing or perform better. However, if you already do these things well (or are on your way to proficiency), this book will show you how to get maximum impact and sell your abilities to those who can help you the most, your network.

2. **The most important ingredient for successful networking is simply being the kind of person that other people want to help to succeed.** Your motives have to be positive, real and honest — so do you.

The first point is fairly self-explanatory, and it's related to timing. If the time isn't right for what you're doing or promoting, all of your work and hard-won alliances can be for naught. In the music business you're only as hot as your current project. If you use networking techniques to get in the door and then have a mediocre product, you have no future credibility. Wait until you have the goods.

Work, improve, get feedback and opinions, but make sure you come in with guns blazing. Your instincts are vitally important, and once you've used your personal networking contacts to give you a fair and unbiased opinion of your product, then hopefully you will also have the judgment to know that the time is right to act.

The second point is a little trickier. It's a fairly consistent rule of thumb in business that in order to get something you have to give something of equal value. For someone just getting started, this reciprocity can be tough — but think hard, because sometimes sharing in your singular sense of positivity and creativity can be all the payback others want or need. Naturalness and warmth are very appealing qualities, even to hardened music industry professionals. If people can help you to nurture your abilities and grow and ultimately share in your success, they will be rewarded emotionally and financially.

Take a critical look at yourself in light of these two points. If you choose to ignore them, you will limit your chances for success.

My Mother Always Said "Life Is Too Short to Spend Around Unpleasant People."

This particular platitude has the ring of truth. It's easy to grouse about the abysmal state of music at any given time, and it's also easy to compare your lack of success to what is successful at the moment, but none of this does any good. We can sit around my living room discussing the negative merits of Michael Jackson's latest release, but be assured, he's not sitting around talking about us, is he? Don't say no with words, say yes with positive actions and an honest and full-out effort to get your music to where you, in your heart of hearts, know it must be. Don't let anyone tell you you can't do this, because only you can determine how far you will go.

It's not just your positivity that will motivate others, it's being able to use that energy to make things happen. No magical person will emerge from the woodwork to wave a wand and make your career successful. This tired myth has to be debunked. Success in the music industry is a result of initiative, control and craft combined with timing, understanding the business, having realistic expectations and networking.

The current music market is very fragmented. Because there is a diversity of musical forms unheard of in past decades, there are more opportunities for musicians and bands that are out of the so called "commercial mainstream." With the tightening of record business economics however, the opportunities are often coming from independent labels who aren't afraid to take chances. In this book we'll discuss how to call attention to what you're doing through self-determination and making your abilities, talents and music clearly visible to your potential network.

WHAT YOU'RE GOING TO LEARN
In this book I'm going to answer questions, debunk myths and relate true examples of success in the music business through networking. My sources are some of the most respected names in the business. By understanding the alliances and career choices made by these successful individuals, you will be able to draw a correlation to your own circumstances, enabling you to take certain actions and make specific career choices. Because you never know when career-making opportunities will occur, one key to future success is to put yourself in a position which will allow career-making events to happen. You must learn to recognize and court valuable relationships.

EVERYBODY WINS
Songwriters need singers, singers need songwriters, both need demos, and studio owners need composite tapes. Performers need videos, and video companies need great-looking performers in the videos they show to future clients. Because everyone needs something, with creative networking it is possible to create a situation in which everyone wins. You can save thousands of dollars through systems of paybacks, barters and trades. In *Networking in the Music Business* I will explore the options and show you how to trade your expertise in one field to achieve what you need in another.

Everyone loves a winner; projects that appear to have backing and momentum will attract individuals hoping to benefit by association. Since many of these relationships can be beneficial to your project, it's important that you learn to make judgments about who can help you and know when to court their favor.

DO YOU NEED TO NETWORK?
In the music business in the last forty years, most major artists and trends have sprung from specific "scenes": from New York's Tin Pan Alley in the 1950s to 1967 Haight-Ashbury in San Francisco, from new wave on New York's Bowery in the 1970s to Seattle, Washington, in the 1990s. Being a part of a scene adds credibility to individual participants, and the media attention makes it all seem bigger than life. The press is much more inclined to write about music that also works on other more complex and newsworthy levels, whether political, social, fashion-oriented or theatrical. In our media-driven society, pop music is certainly one of the most

talked about and written about forms of entertainment. For many bands, being a part of a scene has helped to thrust them into the limelight where they are then allowed to develop their own identity.

If you can't join a preexisting scene, the other option is to develop your own. In *Networking in the Music Business* you'll meet people who've been canny enough to recognize and develop creative outlets for their talents and know how to actively involve other creative compatriots in their game plan.

Creative people suffer if they operate in a vacuum. Though our current technology allows communication through faxes, modems and machines and it is possible to simulate the sound of an entire orchestra in a bedroom through MIDI recording technology, personal relationships have become even more vital. With the development of new technology comes the possibility of involving more people and their talents. Video has blurred the line between rock and roll and filmmaking. Corporate sponsorships and commercial endorsements make the difference between a successful rock tour or one that loses money. Understanding the relationships between these various arts and businesses is vital to all entertainment people in the 1990s, and beyond.

Musicians, songwriters, music business personnel, publishers, producers, students of recording arts, journalists, scenemakers, club owners, agents, managers and anyone else currently involved with or hoping to be involved in the music business in any way need to know how to network successfully.

Personal relationships are the backbone of any business. In the music field, as volatile and shifting as it is, you're going to need some rocks to hold on to. These relationships, and the business you gain as a result of these contacts, will help to anchor you and give you a variety of career options and outlets. It's a growth process; you won't be able to hold on to familiar places or people if you truly want to succeed. You'll have to change, meet new people and know how to make the most of new contacts.

DO YOU HAVE WHAT IT TAKES TO MAKE IT IN THE BUSINESS?

Self-determination, initiative and ambition are mighty tools indeed. The ability to adapt, grow and educate yourself are of vital importance. Schools, classes and books (many by this publisher) address these needs by supplying information to those who need it. Music business aspirants, especially in the performing end, have a limited window of salability. The record charts are now dominated by performers in their early-middle twenties, with performers getting younger and younger. Even the legendary rock bands like the Rolling Stones and Aerosmith are riding on popularity they established at a much younger age. The application of the principles in this book will help you to ascertain exactly what you need to do to achieve personal success in the music business and to maximize your moves within a shorter period of time.

Creating a public persona while working to achieve success is a necessity in an image-conscious industry. Nowhere else do appearances matter so much as in the music business; a personal sense of style is mandatory to create a favorable impression, to add to your recognizability, and to make you memorable. In conventional businesses men wear conservative suits, white shirts and ties; in the record business, such attire would create instant distrust if not dislike. *Networking in the Music Business* will be the first book to discuss these personal visual matters, to analyze them and to offer specific options. It is said that you never get a second chance to make a good first impression. The information in this book will show you how to make the best possible impression on the people who can make and break careers.

SELLING YOUR STUFF

Letters, faxes and telephone conversations are the jungle drums of the music industry. When communicating with your network of sources and contacts, information has to be conveyed in a concise and strategic manner. Many of the skills required for communication are also sales techniques, necessary to convince others to buy your products, concepts and plans. In this book we'll explore the differences between advertising, public relations, publicity and promotion, and fundamental "how-tos" in each of these areas.

Since the proverbial thousand-mile journey begins with a single step, *Networking in the Music Business* is not geared only to readers in the music capitals. Many of the most exciting trends in recent years in the industry have come from nontraditional music cities. With decentralization comes an opportunity for performers and musicians to succeed without having to uproot themselves to go to New York, Nashville or Hollywood. The same principles of networking will adapt themselves perfectly to the local level.

The music business is traditionally a male-dominated field, and women in the record business have often been relegated to publicity and secretarial services. In recent years however, women have begun to make inroads in other areas, specifically in publishing, management and A&R. You'll see how the role of women is changing, and also how other minorities, especially Latinos and Asians, may be able to parlay the multicultural trends of the last decade of the 1900s into lasting success in the music business.

PUTTING IT ALL TOGETHER

Networking in the Music Business is not for dreamers. It is intended as a working guide for anyone who is planning to make an impact in the music business. It is not only hard to break in, it is impossible without specific tools and information. This book delivers a concise and current insider's view, as well as career and motivational blueprints, and eye-opening dialogue with key movers and shakers who have literally changed the face of popular music in our culture.

As you read this book, keep in mind that there is no easy way to succeed. The music business is one of the most, if not *the* most, competitive field in existence. It's also one of the most exciting and volatile fields imaginable, and for those of us who live and breathe it, it's the most important thing there is.

Above all though, none of this would exist without the music itself. As the business end becomes more sophisticated, it's essential that the music that motivates and drives it remains fresh, young and spontaneous. The music should never be determined and directed by those only looking at the bottom line. The music biz is one of the places where the true wild card can emerge: where an unheard-of act can vault to the top of the charts, where an unknown can become a household word in a matter of months.

Behind these successes lies the most important element: the network.

CHAPTER ONE

WHAT IS NETWORKING?

A network is a group of people who provide the framework within which you do business. Networking refers to any contact within that interpersonal framework. In the music business your networking contacts will include producers, musicians, music store retailers, video producers, record and publishing company personnel, talent buyers, club owners, members of the press, and a seemingly inexhaustible list of fellow songwriters, musicians and technicians. It's through networking that all business is done — not only music business but every feasible configuration of commerce.

In the Introduction I told you that success in the music business is determined by three factors. Let's take a closer look:

1. **Who You Know.** Is your uncle the president of a record company? Congratulations, you've already got someone to listen to your tape. But for the rest of us, we'll have to seek out and meet individuals down the long road who can help us get where we're going. And equally important, we have to be able to help them get where they want to go too.

2. **What You Know.** You wouldn't be holding this book right now unless you had a desire to succeed in the music business, so already you have an advantage, not only by reading this book, but by being a person with a quest for knowledge and the desire to fill in the gaps about your chosen profession. Throughout this book I'll suggest ways to educate yourself about the business. Many of these methods are inexpensive or virtually free. You don't need a ton of money to be successful in the music business, but knowledge is power.

3. **Who Knows You.** High-priced entertainers can afford to have publicists working for them full-time, but in the real scheme of things a fledgling music industry professional has to wear a num-

ber of hats, not the least of which is that of the self-promoter. You are your own best representative, and knowing where to go, who to talk to, how to present yourself and how to follow-up is crucial.

When your car breaks down do you thumb through the yellow pages and pick out an unknown mechanic at random? Probably not, because when it comes time to make major purchases we don't always go for the best deal; often we contact someone we know, or someone who has been referred to us. The music business is exactly the same way. It's not the best music that gets recorded, but that which has managed to slip down a well-established pipeline through definable commercial channels to reach a targeted audience of buyers.

Unless you have contacts, your music will never be heard by anyone. You can't hide your light under a bushel. You have to expand and meet others; hence a network.

HOW DO I KNOW THIS IS TRUE?

Coming up as a songwriter, I wrote literally hundreds of songs in different styles, and even had a staff writing deal in Nashville at one point. But it wasn't until I began working with a co-writer who had major contacts that any of my songs got recorded and began to generate income. The songs that made money were not by any stretch of the imagination the strongest songs from an artistic standpoint; however, they were for specific artists that we knew needed songs at that moment (timing), needed the specific style of songs we had (suitability), and that we could get to (networking). One of the songs was recorded by an aging pop/jazz legend; we played the song over the phone for her *hairdresser*, who loved it. We overnighted a tape and lyric sheet to Los Angeles, and the next day, lo and behold, we had a commitment for her to record the song. That's a true story; here's another. I met a publisher at the Songwriters Expo. He had contacts at ABC-TV who required a song about "getting rich quick." He told the network that he had a perfect song; then proceeded to stall them for a couple of hours. In four hours a co-writer and I not only wrote a song, but created an atmospheric 4-track demo for the show. When the publisher turned it in to the show's music producer, he "loved the Randy Newman feel," and the song aired on "General Hospital" repeatedly for about a month, accruing valuable airplay monies for all parties involved.

So let's face it, it's not the best songs or the best acts or the best music that get over, it's the most connected. Rather than mourning this simple fact, get on with it — network. Align yourself with others who are success-oriented and can help you create and market a salable product.

I'VE GOT A GREAT SONG FOR WHITNEY HOUSTON!

As advertising director for the Los Angeles Songwriters Showcase I've met about a zillion songwriters over the last five years. I love writers, neurotic creatures that they are (I include myself here!), but sometimes their expectations are so unreasonable that they border on the bizarre. I'll meet writers who'll play me one of their songs and claim that if they could ". . . only get it to (insert one) Mariah Carey, Paula Abdul, James Ingram, Patti LaBelle, etc.," the artist would love it, cut it, and life would be a beautiful dream o' milk 'n honey.

So you've got a great song for Whitney Houston. My plumber probably has a great song for her too, but the truth of the matter is that Whitney is surrounded by successful people, has access to the best writers in the business, and works with monumental writer/producers who have songs for her too. All the songwriters who have already written chart hits for her have stuff too, plus access and credibility, so where does that leave us? It's astounding how many novices in the music business spend time and money to access the names, addresses and phone numbers of artists' managers and send tapes and letters which go directly in the circular file.

Would you get very excited about a no-name singer without a record deal who's doing a one-shot at a smoky club singing Broadway show tunes? This is exactly who Whitney Houston was when Arista Records brought her to Los Angeles to have her perform at an industry showcase. They invited all the heaviest songwriters in town, many of whom didn't bother to show up. Whitney sang her heart out and the rest is, as they say, history.

One of singer Mariah Carey's most frequent collaborators is a young man named Ben Margulies. He also produced many of the cuts on her first breakthrough album. Was he an established songwriter or producer at the time? No. But he was someone who began working with Mariah when she was only seventeen years old, making little demos in a makeshift recording studio. When Mariah had her shot, so did Ben.

Once people become successful, they have so many middlemen

(and women) creating barriers between them and the world that their existence is isolated and unreal. The demands on their time are intense; access to them is very limited.

The lesson here is to get in on the ground floor, to meet artists when their careers are beginning, be a part of the nurturing and development phase, make yourself an integral part of what they're doing, and expend your valuable energies in the creation of a mutually beneficial relationship.

Instead of craning your neck staring at the stars, begin to look around you, at people you may already know, or situations you can control. Control is one of the most valued commodities in the music business. At the point when you're beginning your career you may not have any money from your endeavors, but you do own everything you create. As you begin to advance your career, elements of your creations are reassigned — a publisher owns pieces of your publishing rights, a record company owns the right to market your music, merchandising companies own the right to market your likeness. From your earnings, you'll pay a manager somewhere around 20 percent, an agent 10 percent of your booking fee, a business manager 5 percent, and a music business lawyer up to 5 percent of your advance funds from the record company.

At the onset of your career then, it's important to have a grasp of the fundamental elements that make up a career, to have strong goals, and to understand that ultimately you'll direct more of your destiny if you're educated and have a strong, positive network of people you can depend on.

LINKED CIRCLES

Your network is really more than just a single group of people. There are many interconnected networks. After a recent concert, I held a reception for my management client. In observing the interaction of the band, musicians, technicians, journalists and assorted party-goers and scenemakers, I saw that the specific networks resembled rings, circles of contacts, that were interwoven and connected. I illustrate it in the diagram on the following page.

All the divergent groups in one physical place are linked through their relationship to the primary event; therefore, each individual member of each network has an opportunity to move freely between interconnecting networks, or circles.

The *artist* is obviously the focal point of this event, and works

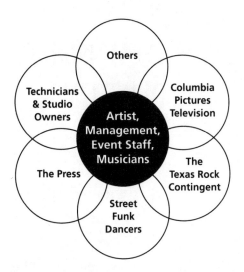

with his *management, the staff* and *the musicians*. One of the musicians is from the *Texas rock contingent* and has invited his friends to the party. Some of his friends are also *technicians* and *studio owners*. The show includes *street funk dancers* who have invited their friends. We used this opportunity to premiere a video (with performances by the artist, dancers and musicians and sound by a technician and studio owner), so the *Columbia Pictures television* people are in attendance. All of this is being observed by the *press*, invited by the *artist* and *management*.

We are all capable of putting ourselves in these kinds of situations. By limiting ourselves to contacts within one small network we are limiting our opportunities, so the goal then is to make new contacts constantly. Meeting new people and establishing new working relationships is the key to a successful career.

Music Biz Myth #1: *All of this networking is OK for some people, but I'm an artist; I like to stay in my space and create.*

The Facts: Creating is wonderful; most people certainly need privacy to do so. Creative people, though, are often neglectful of the most essential elements of commercial enterprise: sales. Selling doesn't have to be sleazy or deceptive; it's simply a new hat that you put on. Networking can be just as creative as writing or recording; instead of working with a sound palette you're working with interpersonal relationships.

CHAPTER TWO

THE MODERN MUSIC INDUSTRY

UNDERSTANDING RELATIONSHIPS IN THE MUSIC BUSINESS

Music industry employees change jobs about as often as most of us change our clothes. It's a constantly shifting panorama with many of the movers acquiring the same or better positions at other companies within the industry. So, it is absolutely necessary that you read the weekly bible of the music industry, *Billboard* magazine, to educate yourself about the business, to keep yourself current, and to begin to understand trends and the economic climate. *Billboard* is expensive to subscribe to (even though it is a legitimate business expense and therefore tax-deductible) but it is available at most libraries.

Now let's consider some of the people you are ultimately aiming for as you network. Specifically, these include A&R reps, music publishers, producers, lawyers, musicians and journalists.

A&R

If you're managing artists, or if you're an artist or songwriter yourself, you will eventually need to deal with the record company's A&R (short for artist and repertoire) department. A&R is the ears of a record label. Employees in this division are typically young, energetic and extremely hard-working. Often A&R people do not have the coveted signing power; however, their endorsement of your music and their unwavering belief in your commercial potential can make the difference in your being signed or not.

A strong commitment and endorsement from A&R is a necessity for any act. Some established acts even have what is known as a "key man" clause in their contract, stating that if their A&R person leaves the company, the act has the option of doing so also.

A rule to remember in dealing with A&R and record companies in general is this: *loyalty is to individuals, not to companies*. To illustrate this point, imagine this scenario. An enthusiastic young A&R person convinces her label to sign a band that she believes in very strongly. She nurtures the band, attends recording sessions, helps them choose songs, and acts as an unofficial den mother for the group. Unfortunately for the act, she is wooed away to another company with the promise of more money and power. The band is still at the original label, but without a champion or any support from the A&R person's successor (who has her own acts to support). The band runs into budget trouble with their recording, and the label, rather than invest any more dollars in the project, refuses to allow them to finish their recording, and puts it on the shelf. The band at this point has three options: (1) They can repay their advance and recording costs and buy back their contract. (2) If they can interest another label in their half-finished project then this label can possibly arrange a "buy-out" of the original contract from label number one. Of course the band shouldn't expect any money in the form of an advance, since company number two is having to pay for what they've already done. (3) The band can wait out their contract, which may be a period of years; then they're free to go elsewhere to sell themselves again.

However, in corporate America it's not enough for your company to make money; your goal is to have the other company lose money. Therefore, to allow the band to go to another label to generate economic gains for that other company would violate this most basic rule of business. In this case a record deal is not the end of the rainbow, it's the beginning of a long nightmare.

What Do A&R People Look For?

This is a subjective question, but the bottom line is A&R reps look for *acts that touch them emotionally and that they know can make money for their companies*. An A&R person's job depends on his or her intuition and many an A&R rep has joined the unemployment lines when a band stiffs. A band with a support network, a strong, knowledgeable manager, a known attorney, a track record of live performances, a great demo tape, a video . . . all of these indicate that the band means business.

Music Biz Myth #2: *"My songs are so good that even recorded on a $25 tape recorder with a handprinted lyric sheet it's obvious I'm a genius."*

The Facts: I meet acts and songwriters with substandard demo tapes, songs, etc., who assume that A&R reps have some remarkable vision that enables them to see beyond such shoddy submission materials. *In order to make yourself signable, you have to appear to be already signed.* Your recordings have to be first rate. Your tapes and lyric sheets have to look professional, like commercially available recordings. Press and bio materials have to be on a level that the label representative is used to seeing and comparable to what their companies generate in their publicity departments. The less work an A&R rep has to do to get your act up to signing level, the easier it is to sign you.

In order to be deemed ready to be signed by a major label you usually have to have a track record locally or regionally, or you've got to come in with a manager or a producer whose credibility is so strong that the label will sign you on the basis of your support team, or you've got to be so fresh and unique that your salability is undeniable. If you don't fulfill at least one of these requirements you're probably not ready for the big leagues yet. But take heart, no one starts at the top, and as the ancient Chinese philosopher said, "The journey of a thousand miles begins with a single step."

I attended a music business symposium recently where a participant on a panel was asked, "How does my act meet A&R people?" The A&R person responded, "Create a buzz, play out. Generate press, reviews and an audience, and we'll find you."

Music Publishers: The New A&R?

With labels tightening up in developing new acts, music publishers have moved in to take up some of the slack. Music publishers help songwriters find outlets for their material. For their efforts, publishers take a percentage of income generated on behalf of the song, including money earned from airplay on radio and television and that earned through record sales (referred to as mechanical royalties). In a business that counts pennies, millions of dollars are made annually.

Typically songs are broken into two pies: A writer owns 100 percent of one pie, the "writer's share," and when he creates the work — if he has no co-writer — he also owns 100 percent of another pie, which is referred to as the "publisher's share." Signing a contract with a publisher is a major step for a songwriter because the publisher's job is to find outlets for songs — to have them commercially recorded and used for profit. For his efforts a publisher is assigned a certain percentage, up to 100 percent, of the publisher's pie. A writer with a track record often owns all or part of his publishing income, a new songwriter may assign all of the publisher's share to a specific company in return for an advance on eventual revenues.

In recent years the trend has been for a publishing company to sign a band and give them money (which can be as little as $100 a week and up to about $500) in the form of a *recoupable* advance. The band can then make demos and theoretically live on the money they're given. They are "in the business," and they have a publisher actively seeking out career opportunities for them, including a record deal, and providing much needed creative and emotional support. Since many publishing companies are owned by or affiliated with record labels, it's possible to sign with a major label via that label's publishing arm.

All of this looks good on paper. The downside is that the publishing income from a hit song can amount to much more than what the publishing company has paid you in return for your publishing. To sign this type of deal, you should not only consult with knowledgeable legal counsel, but also consider your own belief in the long-term financial viability of your work. The bright side to this arrangement is in knowing that a publisher can be a powerful ally. If career development for an artist is in order and you have the interest of a legitimate publisher, then you have a distinct advantage. Many of the current deals for bands who write their own material are co-publishing agreements: The publisher administers the publishing and shares in a predetermined percentage of the 100 percent "publisher share"; the writer then retains a piece of his publishing, in addition to his percentage of the 100 percent "writer's share" pie.

For more on music publishing, read *Protecting Your Songs & Yourself*, by Kent J. Klavens, or *Music Publishing: A Songwriter's Guide*, by Randy Poe, both published by Writer's Digest Books. The bible for songwriters, incorporating everything you need to know, is *The Craft and Business of Songwriting*, by John Braheny, also published by Writer's Digest Books.

Production Deals

Another way into the maze of this record world is through a production agreement. Explained simply, it works like this: an artist signs with a producer. The producer then records the artist and shops the finished product to the record labels, who distribute and market the product. The record label pays royalties to the producer, who then pays the artist. Depending on the clout of your producer and his track record, this method can work for exposing new, unusual artists who wouldn't otherwise have a shot; however, it can also chain artists to producers through control of their recordings, publishing rights to their songs, and management of their careers.

If you choose to work with a producer, always check out his reputation in the industry; make sure that the direction he wants to take you in is compatible with your vision of your music, and that you share a common vision. There is a legal term called *overreaching* which is what happens when a producer or artist manager takes unfair advantage of a novice performer by controlling an unfair share of the recording, writing or performing income. Trust your instincts, and avoid any situation that has this potential.

You should now have some idea of the people you need to ultimately reach in your network and the roles they play. Always contact a reputable music business attorney before signing anything.

CHANGES IN THE MUSIC BUSINESS

In the last five years the record business has become ruled by the giant conglomerates: BMG, Polygram, MCA and WEA. Of these, only WEA is owned by a United States-based company.

The record business then is becoming more international. The U.S. market is shrinking; 30 percent of all records produced and marketed are sold in the U.S., while Europe now accounts for more than 33 percent. The baby boomers, who grew up on rock and roll in the 1960s and 1970s, can fill radio station coffers with advertising dollars, but they're less inclined to buy records. In Mexico and Latin America, the buying demographic is much younger than in the U.S., and in Europe acts that may play clubs stateside might be seen in arenas. In Japan, superstar U.S. acts may perform in arenas, but the record sales are strictly dominated by Japanese artists.

Author/theorist Marshall McLuhan wrote about the "Global Village." As certain parts of the world come together politically and ideologically, there is more opportunity for an open exchange of ideas, cultures and music. Indeed, many of the forms of music that have found their way into the pop mainstream in the U.S. are amazing: reggae, South African township jive, Zulu vocal choirs, Mexican mariachi ballads, the aboriginal sounds of the Australian outback over a driving dance beat. All of these forms have surfaced in the 1990s pop music. The newest thing may well be derived from the most ancient form.

The buyers are also fragmented. New age music, dance, AOR (album-oriented rock), adult contemporary, alternative and urban all serve a specific group of buyers who, fortunately, allow for the economic survival of the individual purveyors of these diverse forms.

Country music has made tremendous strides. The success of performers like Garth Brooks, Travis Tritt, Randy Travis, George Strait and Clint Black has been nothing short of phenomenal. One reason for this success is that the aging baby boomers who no longer relate to rock music still buy records. Country music is now purchased predominately by women, who prefer less truck-drivin' and whiskey-drinkin' songs and more intelligent lyrics.

The man who coined the phrase "country and western" is Cliffie Stone, a legend in country music. Cliffie produced Tennessee Ernie Ford's classic "16 Tons" and has been active in country circles in California for decades. "We have demographics for country we never had," proclaims the ever-talkative Stone, "Fourteen- to twenty-five-year-old kids are treating country shows like rock concerts. The audience for country is changing; they like the story songs and they identify with the simple words."

In the music business timing is vital. Imagine sitting in a record company office in the dark ages before rap, explaining that you wanted to record a type of music that was a form of rhymed speaking over a sampled and synthesized beat with no singing. Think you'd get a record company advance? Rap was manufactured and marketed by its original creators, and found popularity on the street because it had a singular style, fashion and a political and social statement with which listeners could identify. By the time its original producers had made their lucrative distribution deals with the major labels, even white rappers had appropriated and diluted the style (much as they did decades before with "race" records), and you could hear the formerly "gangsta" music being used to sell soda pop on network television commercials.

Rock, in its purest form, is absolute outlaw music. Bands that incorporate a renegade stance are capable of tremendous record sales. From Elvis through the Rolling Stones to the Sex Pistols and Guns N' Roses, the power of rock has always been its incredible ability to polarize its listeners; it's a love it or hate it proposition. Non-mainstream forms like heavy metal, thrash, punk and rap succeed because their practicioners can mirror the specific resentments and rebellion of their buyers: from Bill Haley to Ice-T is a shorter leap than many urban sociologists can imagine.

Rock is the expression of a vital need, a noisy outlet and an elemental outpouring. Those who can channel, recognize and cultivate this essential key will continue to grow wealthy from its exploitation. Today's outlaw form is tomorrow's cornflakes commercial, and as audiences become more deluged by images emanating from every form of media around them, they will require more and greater stimulation just to catch their attention. What was once only visible through smoky glass in a Times Square movie theater is now mainstream entertainment. Welcome to the end of the century.

New forms of global media and a new emphasis on social consciousness can be seen through organizations and events like USA for Africa, Amnesty International, The Freddie Mercury Benefit, Rock the Vote, Rock Against AIDS and the Farm Aid Concerts. Rock, after decades of bloat and excess, is relevant and political again. The bands and entertainers who participate in these events have strong feelings; they also reach a tremendous audience.

Utilize this strategy on a local level to call attention to your music. Rock in the real world is a potent force; in Haiti a song sparked a revolution. Music has the power to bring people together for political thought and change. To quote rock poet Patti Smith, "People have the power."

Music Biz Myth #3: *The Japanese, the Dutch and the Germans control our records.*

The Facts: Mashashita Electronics owns MCA Music; BMG, or the Bertleson Music Group, owns RCA; the Dutch Polygram Company owns Wing, Polygram, Island and a host of other labels; CBS Records is owned by Sony. As we've seen with foreign ownership of the movie studios, though, the end product is not controlled by the parent companies, simply the bottom corporate line. The Japanese companies are very interested in entertainment-related commodities and companies and have acquired many of them during the last five years. No one made these particular companies sell out to the Japanese; it was simple economics, a price was set, a bid was produced.

Given the Japanese record for financial and moral stability, this is probably an improvement over the widespread corruption and greed in certain segments of the industry, but the bottom line is it's a profit machine. The ownership is secondary to its primary function, to make money.

Music Biz Myth #4: *The music business is run by gangsters.*

The Facts: Organized crime has always been a factor in the distribution of goods and services having to do with the entertainment world. The music business is no exception to this, particularly in the realm of record promotion and wholesaling. Periodic payola scandals have rocked the industry since the late 1950s. When these are exposed there is a great outcry and a subsequent purging of key figures; then of course business continues as usual.

The men who a generation ago formed the present-day music business as we know it were certainly not above doing everything within their power to assure the success of their acts. To a certain degree it's the same today. The music business goes by its own sliding sense of morality; a record company president can be fired from his position at one company for phony expense account reporting and be given the presidency of another company a week later. A chief organized crime figure can give potentially damaging testimony before a grand jury only to be welcomed back as an independent consultant.

However, with the corporate takeover of the record business, dealings will be under scrutiny by the corporate office and ultimately by the shareholders of the company. The element of undercover players is certainly diminishing. The use of Soundscan to chart the sale of records in retail outlets is also making certain unsavory elements of the business obsolete.

Women and Minorities in the Music Business

Women. The *Los Angeles Times* Calendar section has a yearly feature that spotlights the fifty most influential people in the music business. This year there was only one woman, Madonna. The music business is notorious for being a male-dominated field. This has always been so, but there are signs that a few things are improving for females.

Historically, women have been relegated to the world of press and publicity. As of this writing, most of the major labels have women in A&R positions on their staffs, indeed, as vice presidents in this position. Unfortunately, women have yet to make inroads into the highest echelons of the music business: The CEOs, the presidents and the chairmen of the boards, with only one exception as of this writing, are men. It's only a matter of time before intellect and resourcefulness win out and more women break this barrier.

In the studio world, women have often been relegated to "talent" or to background vocalists. There are rare exceptions; some of the funkiest bass lines ever created on record were by Carol Kaye, a session bass player. Jennifer Batten, a Hollywood-based metal guitarist, can put 99 percent of the rock players in town to shame. In the world of record engineering and record production, though, the male domination is very obvious.

I spoke with Karen Jackson, of the Hayward, California-based organization Women in Music about this situation. Ms. Jackson feels that it's simply a physical matter — the long, intense hours of the recording studio are easier for men to endure.

Women in the music business are also subject to harassment, a situation which finally came to a head last year with the firings of high-level label personnel, one the president of a major label, who treated his employees disrespectfully. I have a female friend currently on the road as a tour manager for a legendary R&B star who successfully fends off his amorous embraces on a nightly basis. For her to make a scene about this situation would be to risk her job, which she finds lucrative and rewarding.

The flip side of the coin is that even though women represent a small percentage of music industry executives, in just about every genre except hard rock and metal they are the largest buyers of records. Wouldn't it make sense then that women in executive positions could better determine what's a hit than a man?

There is a new national organization forming to help women gain prominence and support in the music industry: Women In Music, 31121 Mission Blvd., #123, Hayward, CA 94544, (510) 471-1752.

Minorities. The music business is a great equalizer in black/white relations. All the great North American music forms, from jazz to rock and roll, have essentially been the grandchildren of black music. Black music continues to provide many of the most innovative records to date, and the trends and fashions associated with these forms influence every segment of our population.

Unfortunately, many times black musicians have been excluded from the rock and roll world and expected to perform only "black" music forms. The Washington, D.C.-based rock band, Living Colour, formed a potent and influential networking/support group, the Black Rock Coalition, to produce shows and compilation albums. The lack of imagination from major label marketing departments is surprising, since music crosses all color lines. Black entrepreneurs, from Motown's Berry Gordy to hip-hop king Teddy Riley, have used their influence to change the course of popular music. Chuck Berry, the father of rock and roll, was not an R&B musician, he was a black rocker.

The pop world retains its strict black and white orientation. Only a handful of Latino rockers have broken through to pop stardom like Ritchie Valens did in the late 1950s. Currently a short list of rappers, including Mellow Man Ace, Kid Frost, Gerardo and a Lighter Shade of Brown, and L.A.'s Los Lobos are visible in North American pop music. We can look at the electronic media to see that Latinos are rarely portrayed in a favorable light; there are a disturbingly few positive role models for young Latinos in the U.S.

Asians, with a fast-growing population demographic, are not represented at all in pop music. Asians, in all of the popular media encompassing film and television, are allowed to be female seductresses, but the males are viewed as sexless mystics or glasses-wearing corporate nerds. This particular ethnocentricity is apparent in total nonappearance of Asians on the pop charts. Only on the new age charts do we see Asian surnames; again, Asian as mystic or synthesizer techno head.

By uniting to overcome the stacked odds, minorities have fertile opportunities to create new scenes, to call attention to their music via sympathetic media, and to make a difference. Pop music success stories will someday exist for all people. As stagnant as the music scene may seem, there is always something new on the horizon, and as we North Americans move inevitably toward the end of the century, multiculturalism as a political, artistic and social movement is bound to influence pop music.

How Do I Find a Job in the Music Business?

You will rarely, if ever, see a record company position advertised in the "Help Wanted" section of a newspaper in New York, Los Angeles or Nashville, because the number of aspirants wanting to fill these jobs greatly exceeds the number of positions available. Even though most record companies don't pay well, especially in the lower echelons, there is still so much magic and prestige involved that these positions are rapidly taken. Generally, interns are used at record companies, free bodies who do a variety of tasks. When paying positions open up, interns are often moved into them.

As record labels have been purchased and assimilated in recent years, many long-term employees have lost their jobs. If stability is needed in your life, you may want to seek jobs in and around the music business which can provide you with this requirement, but very few positions are long-lasting in this turbulent sphere.

Six Ways to Get a Job in the Record Business

1. Be an intern for a label.

2. Develop computer skills; you'll find your employee potential is greatly enhanced.

3. Apply for a mailroom position.

4. Meet promotional representatives from the labels on the local and regional level who can provide a bridge to their companies.

5. Write articles about bands for magazines and newspapers in your area. You'll meet the publicity department and they'll soon have clips of your writing.

6. Promotional jobs at record labels have a high turnover rate. If you're optimistic, energetic and great on the phone, apply to this department.

In this chapter, I've given a brief overview of the current state of the music business and the people who operate within it. In the next chapter, you'll learn how to make contact with these decision makers.

CHAPTER THREE

MEETING THE MOVERS AND SHAKERS

E veryone currently working in the music business must rely on their own network of business associates to help them get their job done. In this chapter, we'll explore ways to contact those networks; we'll consider the networking opportunities in the three music centers (New York, Los Angeles and Nashville); and we'll hear networking tips from some industry heavyweights.

ORGANIZATIONS AND EVENTS
Songwriter organizations exist in virtually every decent-sized city in this country. They are a fertile source for contacts, with not only other songwriters but anyone connected with the business. If NARAS (National Academy of Recording Arts & Sciences, and the presenters of the Grammys) has an office in your region, by all means contact them. Musician unions, though not as powerful as they once were, are still a good source of contacts, too.

Volunteering for music-related events is a sure way to meet key people. Conventions and seminars typically require qualified office personnel, sound people, ticket takers, etc., to run smoothly. You can also work for free admission to these events. Working at philanthropic events enables you to do good work and meet good people.

It is also a distinct advantage to be involved in the organization of an event; this provides you with an opportunity to work with people with whom you wouldn't otherwise come in contact.

A couple of years ago, jazz guitar great Larry Carlton was the victim of a shooting. His first performance, after a long period of recovery, was a benefit held at the Universal Ampitheatre in Los Angeles, for an organization he founded to help other victims of violent crime. Joni Mitchell, Michael McDonald, Lyle Lovett and Michael Franks performed at this event; volunteers included representatives of every major record label and performing rights organization in Los Angeles. The event was hugely successful, not only for Carlton's organization, but for the volunteers, who were there with a common focus and cause and could do some serious networking.

Retail musical equipment stores are frequently a barometer of the music community in a city. When I first moved to Los Angeles, within a week I was hanging out at a local store frequented by many of the top session players in town. By finding out who was who, it became easy to meet some terrifically successful players and to begin to develop relationships that exist up to this day. Many times employees of music stores are also some of the hippest musicians around. They usually have a handle on the needs of the market and who needs musicians at any given moment.

Music business classes at your local college can be hotbeds of ambitious music people. Churches, especially if they have contemporary music, are good places to network in a comfortable and supportive environment. Alcoholics Anonymous's Twelve-Step program is well known in certain parts of L.A. as a great networking opportunity. I know people in town who have never had a drinking problem, but attend meetings regularly in order to pick up contacts!

You need to meet people constantly in order to be successful in the music business. Look for every conceivable opportunity to make your presence known and to become part of your local music scene. It's important to maintain a sense of protocol in all situations where you'll meet industry people. Don't throw tapes in people's faces, don't be obnoxious, but do make an impression as someone they would consider doing business with. Act the part, and act like you know what you're doing.

LONG DISTANCE OR LOCAL?

Without a doubt it's easier to access the people where you live. Trying to establish long-distance relationships with individuals in positions of power, especially at record labels or publishing companies, can be very difficult. However, if you can make regular trips to the music capitals or attend conventions in major cities, these contacts can be parlayed into relationships. At some point in your life you'll need to make a decision whether or not to relocate to a major music capital. Some people spend their whole lives regretting the decision they made to stay in their hometowns; some people regret that they didn't. This is your personal decision, but in this book I'm emphasizing that a lot can be done locally; in fact, from an artist's perspective, it's many times much more advantageous to work in your own area, provided you can build up a substantial following and work effectively to establish your merchandising and recording base before contacting a record label. It is estimated that there are 10,000 rock and roll bands in Los Angeles. Want to make it 10,001? In chapter five there is a section on networking locally which will give you some ideas.

THE MUSIC CITIES

"Nashville, Tennessee, New York and L.A., momma didn't raise her boy to run around this way . . ." — *DK*

For those of you who aren't content to stay at home let's take a look at the three major music centers.

New York is one of the most dynamic cities in the world, its ferocious energy brings out the best and the worst in people. The opportunities it offers are many and varied. The theater world and the jingle industry offer many opportunities for songwriters, singers and actor/singers. The club scene is virtually nonexistent though, except for the "showcase" clubs (read pay to play) and some acoustic venues in venerable Greenwich Village; the jazz scene is good, however, and the rock and roll scene occasionally rises to prominence on the basis of some trend. For session musicians and jazz players, though, New York remains the big time. On the livability scale it's terribly expensive; as of this writing a decent one-bedroom apartment in a tolerable area will set you back at least $1,000 to $1,200 a month. As a crime-infested urban metropolis it's not recommended for the faint of heart, but I learned more about the way the real world functions living in New York than I could have learned anywhere else. It's still the Big Apple.

If You Go to New York:
Songwriters Guild of America
276 Fifth Ave., Suite 306
New York, NY 10001
(212) 686-6820

ASCAP (American Society of Composers, Authors and Publishers)
One Lincoln Plaza
New York, NY 10023
(212) 595-3050

(ASCAP sponsors a highly regarded workshop for songwriters engaged in writing for theater. Call them for details.)

BMI (Broadcast Music, Incorporated)
320 W. 57th St.
New York, NY 10019
(212) 586-2000

New York Chapter of NARAS (National Academy of Recording Arts and Sciences)
157 W. 57th St., #902
New York, NY 10019
(212) 245-5440

Study the *Village Voice* to find the names of clubs, to see what types of music they use, and to see when they hold open mic/ audition nights. The *Voice* also has an extensive musicians wanted section, as well as ads for recording and rehearsal studios.

The Bleecker Street section of Greenwich Village has been a hotbed of musical activity since the 1950s, and it continues today. The clubs on Bleecker, including the Back Fence, Kenny's Castaways and the Bitter End, are great places to begin your search for a musical network in New York.

Nashville, for country musicians, is the best place to live. For musicians working in other forms, however, despite the presence of world-class musicians and studios, it can seem provincial and limited. The live performance scene is virtually nonexistent; however, clubs like the Bluebird Cafe do a great job of uniting the formidable songwriting community through one of the best live songwriting showcases in the country. Some of the best songwriters in the world live in Nashville.

When I first moved to Nashville I was told, "Spend ten years here and you'll be successful." I meet L.A.-based writers who return glowing from song-shopping trips to Nashville, raving about how nice and accessible everyone down there seems. After the glow wears off they realize that, even though everyone was pleasant and though they may have had a good time, they really didn't accomplish anything. Nashville is a very livable city with beautiful scenery, mild winters and even an academic community, but if you're a northerner, a woman, Jewish, Buddhist, black, gay or in any other way different from the norm of the tight white demographics in this town, you may find it rough going. If you do decide to go, take Sherry Bond's book *The Songwriter's & Musician's Guide to Nashville* (Writer's Digest Books) with you.

If You Go to Nashville:
ASCAP
2 Music Square West
Nashville, TN 37203
(615) 244-3936

BMI
10 Music Square East
Nashville, TN 37203
(615) 259-3625

Nashville Songwriters Association International (NSAI)
1025 16th Ave. S., #200
Nashville, TN 37212
(615) 321-5004

NARAS
2 Music Circle South
Nashville, TN 37203
(615) 255-8777

SGA (Songwriters Guild of America)
1222 16th Ave. S., #25
Nashville, TN 37212
(615) 329-1782

Los Angeles can be viewed as a blank canvas on which any picture of one's choosing can be painted. The historical capital of movie-making, L.A., in the 1960s, moved into national prominence as a recording capital. The opportunities are many in L.A. for songwriters, singers and music business professionals. It is a very livable city with terrific weather, and the ocean, mountains and desert nearby. Los Angeles is also a capital of the Pacific Rim, and the opportunities there have attracted people from virtually every country in the world, especially Asians and Latinos.

Californians are amazingly tolerant (though very self-centered), but smog and congestion are constant sources of aggravation. If you're properly motivated and career-oriented, L.A. can be great. The live music scene is limited for paying gigs; for bands it's usually pay to play. There are various scenes springing up all the time though; for example, acoustic music has recently made a strong and welcome comeback. Always the city of the angels.

It's essential to appear successful in this image-oriented environment, because the starving artist routine doesn't cut it here. Creative part-time jobs are plentiful. Tip: Spend money on your car and hair, not your apartment.

If You Go to Los Angeles:

Call The Los Angeles Songwriters Showcase to see who the guests will be at their weekly industry showcase. For twenty-one years this event has given songwriters a place to meet and an unprecedented opportunity to have their songs heard, via tape, by music industry pros. Hint: This organization always needs qualified volunteers in the office, at their weekly events, and at their annual Songwriters Expo, held in the fall.

LASS
P.O. Box 93759
Hollywood, CA 90093
Location: 6381 Hollywood Blvd., #660
Los Angeles, CA 90028
(213) 467-7823

Call the National Academy of Songwriters (NAS) to see what they have going on. NAS is also a nonprofit educational organization which has pitch sessions, seminars and classes. They can also use qualified volunteers.

NAS (National Academy of Songwriters)
6381 Hollywood Blvd., #780
Los Angeles, CA 90028
(213) 463-7178

Call The Songwriters Guild of America. The Guild's popular "Ask-A-Pro" sessions can put you in instant contact with the music industry.

SGA
6430 Sunset Blvd.
Los Angeles, CA 90028
(213) 462-1108

Call the National Academy of Recording Arts & Sciences L.A. Chapter. NARAS presents educational forums for the music industry on a regular basis. They have full and associate member-ships, and have expanded their services for members.

NARAS L.A. Chapter
303 N. Glenoaks Blvd.
Burbank, CA 91502
(818) 843-8233

Los Angeles Women in Music
8489 W. Third St.
Los Angeles, CA 90048
(213) 653-3662

Pick up a copy of *Music Connection Magazine* at any newsstand to get a feel for the musical climate of this town. *MC* also has the best free musician's classifieds going. *BAM Magazine,* available free at music and record stores, covers the rock and roll community; it also provides club listings and classifieds.

Any time you move from the confines of a small community to an urban center there is the inevitable feeling of being the prover-bial little fish in the big pond. Keep in mind though that these media centers are made up of people like you, who had to leave their hometowns to succeed. Also, be sure to reward yourself psy-chologically for what you've already achieved: You've separated yourself from the baggage of your past and actually done what many aspirants never even attempt—you've left home. Keep your expec-tations realistic, set goals, don't expect overnight success, don't arrive in your new location destitute, research your move and, if possible, make contacts before you go. Once you arrive, the very first thing you'll need to do is begin setting up your network.

CRUISING FOR A SHMOOZING

On a warm spring day I walk through Hollywood to Crossroads of the World, a 1930s office complex designed to look like a cruise ship in port. Only in Hollywood! I'm going to meet with Terri Man-dell, the owner of a PR agency called the Mulholland Group. For the last couple of years Terri has been teaching a course on what she refers to as "Power Shmoozing." Shmoozing is an intense form of networking that takes place at gatherings, conventions, parties and anywhere else that people come together en masse for the purpose of making networking contacts. Terri has lectured at the Songwriters Expo in Los Angeles and teaches classes regularly through the Information Exchange, an educational outlet.

D.K.: *If I walk into a room full of hitters who am I going to talk to, what am I going to talk about?*

T.M.: The first thing you have to do is get out of the hitter and nonhitter mentality because most people have trouble talking to anyone. When you focus on, "I only want to talk to the person with the most expensive suit and the most expensive car at this party," it'll trip you every time because that's when all of the fear and intimidation kicks in. So the first thing you have to do is try to equalize everybody and practice on nonintimidating people.

What I teach is complete irreverence and rule-breaking. Here's an example: My husband and I went to the Key Arts Awards for the *Hollywood Reporter*. We went there to schmooze like crazy. So we're standing there and here's these three heavy hitters — Armani suits, ponytails, the whole thing — and my husband walked right up to them and said, "You guys look pretty important, you look like someone I should know, My name's Jim Mandell, who are you?" You need a sense of humor and irreverence — get all the pretension out of the way, be disarming.

Songwriters and music people have such an S&M mentality, but you don't want to come across like a nerd and stick your tape in someone's face; you can't be needy. Try to approach people as equals. In order to do it this way you've got to have patience — give yourself a year and find ways to meet people through the backdoor. The front door is you call them, you send tapes, you leave messages with their secretaries. The backdoor is you hang around the places these people hang around in their non-industry hours, such as fundraising events for their children's schools, or you go to things like political gatherings and environmental groups, and you end up eating dinner beside this person. You're then viewed as a member of the in-crowd, not as some songwriter crawling on your knees up to him. Give yourself six to twelve months to build this plan. How can you go if you can't afford $500-a-plate dinners? You get involved with the group as a volunteer and you work your way in.

One secret about networking is this: You only have to meet as many people as possible; it doesn't even matter who they are. If you get that kind of momentum going in your life, the people you meet will lead you to others who'll lead you to others, etc.

If you as a creative person start doing interesting things, you create bridges for yourself. Create interesting activities — teach a class, write a book — don't be some guy who sits in his house and writes songs. A guy with a tape doesn't work. A guy with a tape who does organic gardening and is writing a book about motorcycle repair is something different. Make yourself more interesting.

D.K.: *What should you wear? How should you look?*

T.M.: My theory about that is you should stand out by not dressing in the uniform. For me, if I see a guy in a leather jacket, earrings, spike hair, I know he's a musician; it doesn't impress me. I think somebody that dresses kind of grown-up has a better effect. To combine the hip stuff with something kind of business-like works better than the rock and roll costume, which just says you're playing the game.

D.K.: *What attracts us to other people in a networking situation?*

T.M.: Sometimes we're attracted to nonthreatening people, sometimes we're attracted to the most powerful person in the room; some people spend their whole night talking to the waiter. What pulls people in is a sense of humor, lightness, looseness. When you see someone who looks comfortable, it's real attractive, being verbal, being alive. The physical thing is very interesting — find the person you trust most in the world and ask for a critique of your physical presence. People don't know they have bad habits. If you ask a friend, a friend will tell you. Touching is real good; when you exit a conversation touch, shake hands, so they don't feel you're deserting them.

D.K.: *How do you tell if other people are ready to exit a conversation with you?*

T.M.: They stop looking at you and start looking everywhere else. You know it's time to wrap it up. If it's you, the best way to escape is be honest — don't worry about someone else's feelings — tell the truth. "You know it's been nice talking to you, I'm going to go on and work the room a little now," is better than "I have to go to the bathroom" (because they might wait for you to return) or "I see someone I know" or "I'm going to get a drink." Telling the truth is the only thing that works. In a mingling situation you'll spend about ten minutes with someone. You have ten minutes to make your presentation and you've got to tell your whole story.

D.K.: *What's a good opening line?*

T.M.: People seem to think it's tacky to ask, "What do you do?"—that it's a pickup line or something. I don't believe that. Be real direct, "Who are you? Why are you here?" It's an OK thing to say. The only people who hate this question are the people who aren't doing anything. We have these notions of what's proper, and this is all wrong.

D.K.: *How does it differ if you're approaching a group of two or three people?*

T.M.: One of the rules we're taught as children is not to interrupt. In networking with groups you're allowed to break in but only if it's three or more; if it's two people, they may be talking about something personal. You have to realize that a lot of events are for meeting people and not be embarrassed by that. You hover around groups, eavesdrop, and if you can hear something you relate to, throw in a comment. They'll either respond or not; you then move in on the group. It's uncomfortable but march up to the group, wait till there's a lull and introduce yourself—casual as can be.

D.K.: *How can you hone your verbal skills?*

T.M.: There are these things I call everyday dress rehearsals. It's just like playing an instrument; practice having conversation with strangers on elevators. Talk to people at the carwash, in line at the bank. It's a normal thing to do; it's not a big deal, it's what people are supposed to do.

The following lists are part of Terri's class and are also included in her book *Power Shmoozing*. I gratefully acknowledge her generosity in allowing me to include them here.

Behaviors, Attitudes and Styles That Push People Away
1. Smoking
2. Drunkenness
3. Sloppy appearance or bizarre fashion statement (acceptable in some circles)
4. Hostile or depressed disposition
5. Excessive profanity (acceptable in some circles)
6. Bad jokes, especially sexist, racist or lewd
7. Talking too much
8. Talking too little

9. Too much hype and jive
10. Bad manners
11. Offensive smells (too much perfume, bad breath — ask your friends!)

Behaviors, Attitudes and Styles That Draw People In

1. A great, but not overbearing, sense of humor
2. Good manners
3. Confidence
4. Nonthreatening appearance
5. Smiling and eye contact
6. Starting a conversation instead of waiting for someone else to do it
7. Knowledge about the subjects at hand
8. Knowing when to let go
9. Not taking yourself too seriously
10. Fearlessness
11. Respect for cultural differences

Basic, Old Fashioned (But Extremely Important!) Rules of Etiquette

Don't interrupt.
Say please and thank you.
Don't be late (it's rarely fashionable).
Always RSVP . . . on time.
Look into the eyes of the person you're talking to.

Tips for Engaging People in Interesting Conversations According to Terri Mandell

Open by commenting on any shared reality you can find: "Are you a member of this organization?" "Isn't this building beautiful?" "Can you believe the traffic out there?"

Use multilayer sentences, and end with a question. Example: "No, but I'm interested in their work and I have a friend who's a member. She said it was a great group with good networking opportunities, so I thought I'd check it out. How about you?" Contribute a lot to the conversation.

Tell the truth: "I'm a studio owner trying to expand my business, so I'm here to hopefully meet some new clients." Or, "I'm newly separated and it's really lonely out there. I'm trying to meet as many people as I can."

Have a sense of humor: "I took a self-improvement seminar that gave us a homework assignment to meet three new people per month, and you're one of them!" It's a lot like telling the truth.

Get to the point and tell everything.
She: My company is introducing a new soft drink aimed at affluent yuppies.
He: Really? You know, I worked on the ad campaign for Blarto Beer last year. I've done a lot of new product introductions in the beverage market.

Create an opportunity for a second encounter. You don't have to close a deal on the spot; just create an on-ramp, which you can complete later on in the party, or on another day.

Give the person something to remember you by — an interesting company name, a funny story that relates to something they're doing, a memorable business card, brochure, newspaper clipping or other "take home" item.

". . . IN THE MUSIC BUSINESS YOUR DESIRE TO SUCCEED HAS TO BE GREATER THAN YOUR FEAR"
— #1 Hit Songwriter Allan Rich

When I asked Allan Rich if he would like to share his experiences in this book he was very receptive despite his demanding schedule as a much-in-demand writer. Allan has been in Los Angeles since 1980 and has written hits for top artists, including Patti LaBelle, Whitney Houston, Gladys Knight, Natalie Cole and James Ingram. Probably best known for Cole's "I Live for Your Love" (co-written with Pam Reswick and Steve Werfel) and "I Don't Have the Heart," #1 for James Ingram (with co-writer Jud Friedman). Allan lives in a charming, woodsey house high in Laurel Canyon in the Hollywood Hills. Over tuna salad he shared some thoughts and played me some new songs that are in various stages of being recorded.

"I was working in Venice Beach, part time, selling Capezio shoes. My friends who owned the store told me about a successful producer/writer, Howie Rice, who had bought ten pairs, and they said the next time he came in they'd introduce me. He came in for the eleventh pair and I was his salesman. I gave him a tape and a couple of weeks later at 3:00 A.M. he called to say how much he liked the songs, and to keep in touch. When I tried to reach him again it was impossible; so I figured, hmm, if he called me late at night he's probably a nightowl, so I called him at midnight. I thought, the worst that can happen is he'll be pissed off, but I can't reach him anyhow, so I may as well give it a try—I don't have much to lose at this point. He answered the phone himself, and things started happening for me. *If I hadn't gotten over my fear and made that call, my life would be very different today.*

"I try to find a way to make people say yes, once they've already said no," Allan laughs, and gives this example. "I'd pitched four songs to Patti LaBelle for her next album, and she'd put them on 'hold,' so I respected that and didn't play them for anyone else. I was in England at dinner and someone at the table said, 'Did you hear? Patti LaBelle finished her album.' I was devastated. When I went back to L.A., I wrote Patti a letter and let her know how disappointed I was that she'd held the songs, not recorded them, and hadn't told me. A couple of nights later the phone rings and it's Patti! She let me know that the record had gone over budget, etc., but she still loved the tunes. We'd cut the demos in her key, so my co-writer Allan Roy Scott and I took the tracks to Patti's hometown, Philadelphia, bumped up to 24 track and recorded her vocals. We used our own money, about $4,000, and they put the two songs on her album."

Nowadays, Allan's reputation allows him almost unlimited industry access, but as he explains, "It's still a 'screen test' each time; it's still about rejection. You've got to put your ego on the back burner, or to quote Quincy Jones, 'Check your ego at the door.'" To young writers who would like to work with him, Allan explains, "I got to write with Burt Bacharach which was a thrill. My publisher (MCA Music) set it up. I met my collaborator Jud Friedman through his publisher at Peer Music. She called me and said, 'We've just signed a new writer. He's never had a cut, but I think he's great. Would you like to meet him?' The first song we wrote together was 'I Don't Have the Heart.' I have a 'hit list' each year of co-writers I'd like to work with; maybe I'm on someone else's hit list."

Barry Manilow was one of Allan's first big-time collaborators.

The two met through Howie Rice, who was working on Manilow's album. Rich was asked to write a lyric to a melody they had, which he labored over. "Then I go to Barry's house with this lyric, which is a trip because I'm still selling shoes at the beach. I walk in the house and find out that they've changed the whole melody; now the lyric won't work. So they send me home to rewrite. Barry is so jazzed by the melody that he's going to record the next day, but I've got a wedding that night, and the next day (Sunday) I've got to work selling shoes, which Barry knows about. So I go to the wedding, stay up till 3:00 A.M., finish the lyric, slide it under Howie's door, and go to work. They call me later to come down to the studio after work. I get there, Barry comes out of the vocal booth and says, 'You wrote a good lyric, now teach me the bridge.' The song is going to be included on a Barry Manilow retrospective."

Another fortuitous job for Rich was as a waiter at the Source restaurant in Los Angeles, a music industry health food hangout. "I'd just start talking to people. I'd meet other writers, tell them what I did. I used to wait on Syreeta Wright. A couple of years later I was in the studio and she was recording one of my songs. I said, 'Do you remember me?' She was amazed. I used to be her waiter, and here she was singing my songs.

"One key is to talk to and be friendly with everyone. *You never know who you might be talking to who could change your life, so let everyone know what you do.* Also be sure to never write anyone off. The person you may be talking to today who you perceive as being nowhere could have a huge hit tomorrow; you just never know."

Allan Rich's personality is an interesting dichotomy as well as a key to his success. On one hand there's the persistent (but never pushy) networking, business-oriented songwriter. On the other hand there is a very warm, open honest, vulnerable artist who believes that his greatest strength is in "being able to say something straightforward which touches people." Certainly his hit songs all have this quality. He is also a tireless worker, someone who understands how the business works, and who enjoys being part of the process. He is very involved in business decisions made by his publisher, and even though he is co-published by a major publishing company, Allan takes the initiative and responsibility for procuring his own cuts and charting his own course.

"You have to make it happen," Allan notes. He certainly does.

THE MUSIC BUSINESS ATTORNEY: DONALD PASSMAN

I am proud to have written one of the very first reviews of Donald S. Passman's book, *All You Need to Know About the Music Business*. When writing the review, I contacted the L.A.-based lawyer, and invited him to speak at the annual Songwriters Expo, which he did, eloquently, to a room packed with rapt listeners.

A soft-spoken, straight-talking, bespectacled Texas native, Passman has represented superstar clients like Quincy Jones, Don Henley and Janet Jackson; he's also negotiated some of the biggest record deals of all time. I met with Don in his office in the heart of Hollywood.

"I was around music all my life. My stepfather was a disc jockey, I played accordion in high school, then I started playing guitar. When I was in college and law school, I played in bands; when I started practicing law, I actually made more money playing in bands, but I wanted to find a way to eat regularly and be in the music business, so I decided to go into the business side. Now I play for my kid's campouts!

"After college I came back to Los Angeles. I started out life as a tax lawyer; then I took a class at USC on the music business (which I now teach) and that was fun. So I changed jobs and went to this firm, twenty years ago. It's still as much fun as it was that first day.

"As it happened this firm represented more companies than artists, so I was representing record companies; then I started doing artists. It was a gradual process to find clients. Our firm's philosophy has never been volume. We look for people we like and can develop a long-term relationship with. We keep it small.

"I have some clients who don't particularly look for commercial success; they want to be true to their art. I think with people like that you get the deals that are consistent with who they are. You don't go out and try to maximize the dollars; you put them with a company who understands their vision.

"By the time I got in the business my stepfather was out, so the only person I knew was (record producer) Snuff Garrett, a client of this office. In a sense, when I came here to work, I immediately got immersed in the business and there were relationships I could plug into. *Aside from that, I made it a point to go out and meet people my age who were doing what I was doing; my theory was, as it has happened, that in twenty years they'd be in very important positions.*

"Speaking specifically, I think that you should pick people who are doing what you want to be doing; you need to get around them to see how they do what they do. If you can't get to them, you can get to people who work for them. Remember, everybody was nobody at some point, no one had heard their name. You want to get out and meet as many people as possible. Some of the people you meet may be of little use to you (though they may be nice people!). You can make some friends, but you never know where some kind of a clue is going to come from. You've got to be aggressive about following up; you've got to be aggressive about chasing things that look promising. It's like fishing: Most of the time you sit there with your hook in the water; every once in a while you might pull one in, or a shoe, or an old tire, but sometimes you catch a beauty, so you've got to invest what you've got the most of which is time. If you want to be an artist, you've got to be out in the clubs, not to copy but to see how it works, who is making it and why. You've got to study it like you'd study anything else. It's like if you were going to be a plumbing contractor, you'd go and watch the contractors. Same thing in the music business. Read interviews, see how people got started; but remember, some of it's press hype. Look for names of people in the business; don't be shy about mailing things to people. It just takes time, so don't get frustrated. Set a reasonable time frame for yourself.

"The one common trait I'd put on all the superstar clients I have is persistence. They're all very driven, very focused. They have a vision of who they are, what they want to be, how they'll get there, and they'll walk through walls to get to where they want to go. They'll pick themselves up if they fall down, and walk around the barrier. And that's the quality that it takes, even more so than talent; it's persistence.

"Meet everybody you can, be nice to everyone, because you haven't a clue; even someone who may not be a direct help to you may have information you can use. It's not necessary to step on other people or to hurt other people in order to be successful. It's better karma if you don't. You'll last longer, have a happier life and sleep better. At the same time, being out there and being part of the group energy keeps you involved. Stay away from negative people, stay where the sun shines. The sleazes never ruled this business. They may have glommed onto a few artists early in their careers and sucked the life out of them for a period of time until the artists wised up and moved along with their lives. While there may have been guys who were aggressive or did things not everybody approved of, they were never slimeballs; they were small players, because when you think that way you stay small.

"Everybody who goes into a new business does it without knowing everything. And a lot of the people who grow up in the business aren't successful, so it's not such an advantage to know everything about it; of course you do need a copy of *All You Need to Know About the Music Business*! But you don't have to be well connected, just talented and persistent.

"It's possible to work on the regional or local level, but if you're going to play in the big leagues, you may want to have representatives in L.A., New York or Nashville. More and more managers are based out of other cities; it's not necessary to live here, but it's necessary to visit here regularly to be in the business.

"The irony of this business is that people are always looking for talent; the perception is you can't get in the door, and in some ways this is a reality. A record company can get five- to six-hundred tapes a week from unsigned bands, hopefuls, and most of the labels won't listen to them if they're not submitted by someone they know. On the other hand, everyone's looking for real talent, and if you're talented and persistent, you're going to make it in the business.

"The Songwriters Expo, USC classes, City of Hope . . . anything you can do and anywhere you can go to meet people and get your name out is positive. The more you're around the better off you are. If it's not your personality, hook up with a manager who's aggressive. You can have the best product in the world, but if you can't get it out there, no one will know."

In this section we've learned about the many networking opportunities that are open to all who care to apply, and we've seen how some successful participants in the music business have established their careers through successful networking. In the next chapters of this book we'll examine you and your personal goals, needs and aspirations. We'll take a look at what you have that can help you succeed as well as what may be holding you back.

CHAPTER FOUR

WHAT HAVE YOU GOT?

SELF-DETERMINATION, INITIATIVE AND AMBITION

I was fortunate to have the opportunity to take a course in artist management from one of the best: Ken Kragen, who has guided the careers of Kenny Rogers, Gallagher, Travis Tritt, Lionel Richie and Olivia Newton-John. A well-spoken, intelligent man, Kragen certainly dispels the unsavory image of the cigar-chomping, back-room hustler. He also organized two monumental charitable events, We Are The World and Hands Across America.

One of the first things Ken had our class do when we arrived at UCLA was to make two lists: the first was a list of things we most like to do; the second, things we least like to do. Initially this exercise felt silly and sophomoric, but it gradually dawned on me what I was supposed to be learning from this exercise: to be able to find and establish a niche in the entertainment world based on these likes and dislikes.

Kragen taught tough self-determination. In the music business you have to be your own boss, and totally in control of your own destiny. For artists, believing that managers are somehow employers who will tell you what to do and provide you money to do it is a ludicrous and erroneous assumption. Indeed, in Kragen's class at UCLA there was a recording legend who had always been told what to do by her managers; millions of record sales later she still needed to learn more about the business which had made her, and her managers, wealthy.

For the fledgling entrepreneur there is no patter to follow. In order to succeed you must chart your own course.

LONG-TERM GOALS

It is absolutely imperative that you write down your long-term and your short-term goals. Until you have set down this information in a form you can see, it will never be real to you.

Keep a notebook or folder with lists, goals and objectives. No one else need ever see it. Your notebook will keep you on track and informed about where you need to be, what you should be doing, what's working and what's not.

Your long-term goals should be everything you hope to do in the future. If you want to be rich and famous, fine; write it down. If you want to be bigger than Elvis, put that down; president of Warner Brothers Records? No problem, put that down too. This list is for you — it's not for anyone else to look at, experience or imagine. Dreams are wonderful things. It's dreams that allow us to see the big picture; goals are simply dreams with deadlines.

Determining your long-term goals can prove to be a daunting experience, because you have to be absolutely truthful with yourself; there is no self-deception allowed. If you are a performer you know what makes your audiences respond. Can you make an audience crazy? Will young girls (and boys) buy your records, put your picture on their walls, dream about you? Buy your records, T-shirts, posters?

If you aspire to the business end of music, can you withstand the pressures involved in making million-dollar decisions? Can you look at the big picture and direct a team of people to do your bidding? Can you sit down with the president of a major record label for a power breakfast and not choke on your napkin? Do you look, talk and act the part? Are you capable of recognizing, managing, channeling, developing and ultimately controlling talent? Are you aggressive enough to go all the way for what you know you deserve?

What do you like to do? Do you need security, comfort, a home life that's relatively normal? There are positions in the music business that allow for this type of serene existence, but they're certainly not the norm! The entertainment world in general runs on an amazing amount of energy, long hours, crazed conditions and a phenomenal amount of travel. All these factors make for a harried existence. Job security is virtually nonexistent. The money paid to employees by record companies is shamelessly small, but so many people want the few available positions. To be in the music business you've got to understand it's more than an occupation. It is more akin to a fever, one caught early in life. Those of us who can change and adapt with the business, will ultimately succeed.

You will find the answers to many important questions as you begin to develop in your career, and you'll find these answers quickly, because the music business, like most of life, is certainly not a spectator sport; you'll have to participate. "You either do it or you don't, trying doesn't count," says record company president David Geffen.

How Do I Determine What I Should Focus On?

Determining whether to be a performer, a writer or a business person is a crucial decision; in order to pursue your aspirations you must first define them. To recognize your strengths, let's take a realistic look at your abilities.

Five Questions for Artists

1. Have I developed a recognizable musical style that is uniquely my own?

2. Am I more than a sum total of my influences?

3. Have I written songs which are better than what I hear on the radio? Have I found songs to sing which no one else can interpret with my feeling and style?

4. Am I being challenged by working with musicians who are better than me, from whom I can learn?

5. Am I spearheading my entire existence around the fulfillment of my musical vision?

Five Questions for Future Moguls

1. Can I recognize talent in others?

2. Do I have a distinct vision?

3. Will others take me seriously as a business equal?

4. Can I see the big picture?

5. Am I spearheading my entire existence around the creation of a network which will help me to fulfill my economic vision?

As you begin to focus on the most important of your goals, you'll have to decide what is attainable, and why you deserve it. Rock and roll heros are people who have no alternative except to do what they do. Can you imagine Axl Rose as a bank teller? Bruce Springsteen selling insurance? If your career goals are more modest or focused on becoming a supporting player, you may have a better chance of fulfilling your aspirations. But you'll never be a rock star, because to do this you absolutely have to be willing to put it all on the line—to sacrifice any type of normal existence, to starve, to sleep on floors, to be treated like dirt for the fulfillment of your music. I don't claim this is exactly how it will happen to you, simply that you have to be ready to do whatever it takes.

I remember my father encouraging me to finish college so I'd have something to fall back on. I resisted this advice because of career opportunities, and I've never once regretted this decision. Know why? In my experience people who have something to fall back on always fall back. In the competitive environment of the music business you'll have no room to fall back. Never in twenty years in the music business have I been asked if I have a college degree. I lecture at UCLA and write books, too.

Diversity is another asset altogether, one that can serve you well in attaining your goals. Although I began as a performer, I am now a manager, publicist, author and public relations consultant. Many people in positions at record companies play instruments, and were drawn to their current vocations because of a love of music developed when performing in fledgling teenage rock and roll bands.

Certain forms of destiny are out of our hands. Since this is not a book on religious science I'll keep my observations earthbound, but one vital key to success is to always be open to new experiences. Don't be close-minded to opportunity when it knocks.

SHORT-TERM GOALS
It is imperative that you plot your course with a series of goal lists. A one-year plan, a six-month plan and a weekly plan work best for me, but you may be oriented to different time increments. Put the most important things to do at the top of your list, and check them off as they're done.

Weekly
Weekly goal lists should be the map of everything you do connected with your career, e.g., rehearsing your band, choosing material, going to your voice lessons, reading business-related materials, networking with other performers or business types, making necessary telephone calls, choosing pictures or costumes, sending press releases and letters of inquiry, and attending auditions. Even though some of the items you include on your list may seem trivial (and you should include absolutely everything related to your career), they're not because everything you accomplish is a small

victory, and it's the small victories that add up to big gains. It also will give you a sense of accomplishment to look over your list and see what you've completed. Sometimes you'll deserve a pat on the back, and finishing your list can help you to feel better about what you're doing, as well as feeling better about yourself; you're laying the groundwork for what must be done.

At the end of the week, look at what hasn't been done and either (a) put it on next week's list, or (b) determine that it's not that important in the first place. Be wary though if you have a number of unfinished items; it could mean that you're not working hard enough or that your goal-setting is unrealistic.

Below is a set of goals, or objectives, for one week in the management of an artist's career. This particular week we were preparing for a show; not every week is this intense.

Week 8/12-8/19
- Letter/tape/press kit to Earthbeat Records
- Package/videotape to Reno promoter
- Call Frankie T /WB Entertainment follow up show invitation
- Melani from Island Records follow up show invitation
- Tape to "On the Boulevard" magazine re: concert review
- Finish choreography
- Rehearse dancers on new routines
- Check with merchandising company to make sure T-shirts are ready
- Create & duplicate flyers for the show
- Meeting with band drummer & new percussionist
- Finish demo of new song
- Complete demo tracks for dance rehearsals

Monthly
Monthly goals should be related to a more comprehensive agenda: ongoing press and public relations campaigns, creation of mailing lists, advertising efforts, location of venues to perform in, putting together future shows, choosing musicians and setting up monthly rehearsal schedules. Following is a sample month for one of my artists.

Objectives September 23-October 23
- Check band schedules
- Set up rehearsal for October 7 or 8, one four-hour rehearsal

- Check out new rehearsal facility
- Get video from the director
- Watch/critique video
- Write raps/patter for show
- Set up appearance for benefit for Kaua'i Relief efforts
  call Larry Wong for concert information
  call Bobby Chun for press releases
- Write press release for Watts 3rd World Festival
- Call the promoter for a list of other performers
- Design a flyer with press quotes
- Do 500-piece mailing
- Write/send/follow up press releases for show
- Music Connection Magazine
- LA Weekly
- LA Reader
- Contact A&R from labels with acts on show
- Follow up calls
- Interscope Records
- Criterion publishing meeting
- Arrange lunch meeting with lawyers
- Dance rehearsal for new routines

Yearly

This is a much bigger picture. If you can tie these goals in with your New Year's resolutions more power to you. They could include: procuring a record deal, a publishing deal, a management contract; becoming more visible in your local market; or relocating to another city where the musical opportunities are greater.

Following is a one-year goal list for a client. Note that there are not as many items on this yearly list as on the weekly or monthly lists, because the yearly goals are much more ambitious and far-reaching. This list provided an overview for the entire year's activities and helped us to move the artist's career in the right direction.

Goals for the Year
- Finish four songs, mastered on 24-track
- Design J-card cassette insert for product; duplicate tapes
- Design new press kit
- Photo session for head shots
- Perform at five high-profile outdoor summer festivals

- Design merchandising campaign for live performance, T-shirts, caps, etc.
- Produce a video
- Package and find outlets for video with local television stations in California
- Find legal representation
- Expand network to include more A&R
- Meet more publishers/find possible film & TV outlets for songs
- Go out to more music industry events
- Do everything in our power to make this act more signable

If you have a partner, a manager or someone you can trust, then these goal-setting techniques will be doubly effective. In order for goal-setting to succeed there has to be some type of accountability. If you're extremely motivated and disciplined you may be accustomed to being accountable only to yourself. Most of us aren't that lucky though, and it helps to have to explain to a second party why something did or didn't get done. You have two options if you're working alone: You can either check off the items yourself on your list, or ask a close friend, spouse, paramour or confidant to be your conscience. Checking off career-related goals as you accomplish them is very rewarding emotionally and will keep you on the road to success.

ELIMINATE THE NEGATIVE

Fear of Failure

To build skills that will enable you to make contact with others, you must recognize and control your fear. It's not the fear that a singer gets before going onstage or fears of tangible things — it's a deep-rooted insecurity that all of us have had since we were children.

In a networking situation the following factors can cause fear:

1. Perceived lack of skill
2. A need for approval
3. A distorted perception of reality
4. A poor self-image
5. Negative self-talk

When you lack skill you lack confidence and therefore feel fear.

What do you need to learn to be comfortable with others in a music business setting? Is it knowledge about the business? Acquire it. Do you feel inadequate about your lack of success compared with others? Maybe what you're feeling is simple envy. Recognize this for what it is and let it flow through you. It's natural.

The need for approval is one of the most basic requirements of all entertainers. The rest of us, to varying degrees, have this trait as a holdover from childhood. When we meet others they may or may not accept us, based on a variety of perceptions, not all of them under our control. How do you feel when an initial contact isn't friendly? Is it reasonable to expect all of our unknown contacts to be so? Do we need to change our expectations regarding approval?

It is very easy to prejudge people we have not yet met. Indeed, we can talk ourselves out of success by imagining all types of negative responses to our efforts to gain a solid footing in the music industry.

Do you often perceive indifference as rejection? It's not; it's a reaction you get from preoccupied or overworked individuals. Don't take it personally, because their reaction has nothing to do with you, simply with the circumstances in which you interact.

I wish I had a dollar for every time someone said to me, "I called _____ Records (insert Capitol, Geffen, Warner Brothers), and the receptionist was very rude when I asked if they listen to unsolicited material!" The receptionist wasn't being rude; she was probably dealing with fifteen other incoming telephone calls and didn't have time to explain to a novice songwriter how the music industry works. Some songwriters seem to think that everyone in New York, Nashville or Los Angeles is dying to hear their material. A vague egotistical overstatement of "how much money your company will make" off these as yet unproven works of commercial artistry only identifies the speaker as a rank amateur.

Networking is the way to get songs listened to, not blindly calling up and bothering record labels or publishing companies. Because of the potential liability brought about by what are determined to be nuisance lawsuits, most of the big companies won't listen to unsolicited material anyhow. Get it where it needs to go through creative networking.

Rejection Is a Fact of Life in the Music Industry

Songwriters pitch songs to publishers who reject them. Publishers pitch songs to producers who reject them. Producers pitch songs to artists who reject them. Producers and artists pitch finished masters to record companies who reject them, and record companies sell product to consumers who reject them. It's a virtual food-chain of rejection, and it's a fact of life. The first time I heard a record company honcho refer to records as "product," I was shocked. The first time a record company A&R man listened to thirty seconds of my song and gave me the bum's rush, I was indignant. As I look back on the experience, however, this was probably the moment I actually began to comprehend the music business.

In the creation of a popular art form, we have to be constantly aware that we create for a competitive economic marketplace in a specific place and time. If you have pretensions about creating works of art that are beyond such petty economic judgments, you'd better become a poet, playwright or a surrealist painter, not a music industry professional.

Fear of Success

It is much easier to be a failure than to succeed. Fear of success is a self-sabotaging trait that keeps us from achieving our potential. Those who fear success think they shouldn't be doing as well as they're doing right now. They may believe they've been too successful too fast, and tell themselves "this can't last." While many people, including some psychologists, think of fear of success as basically a confidence or self-esteem problem, it's really more deeply rooted than that. The fear of success results from having a preconceived notion of just how difficult things are or how tough it is to succeed. When we don't meet the problems we expected, we achieve more and produce faster.

At first we feel happy and have a great sense of accomplishment. But gradually, if we're suffering from the fear of success, we become anxious. Psychologically we are unprepared to deal with this sudden onset of success. We have too much too fast.

Like other self-sabotaging fears, fear of success usually stems from our youth and the messages we receive from our parents. It can also come from feeling overly respectful of the field in which we work, in our case the music business, and feeling that things are more impossible to achieve than they really are.

We all have a negative voice inside us, an inner critic. It is essential that you recognize this voice for what it is and learn to silence it when necessary. Your inner critic will tell you things like this:

1. Don't bother finishing this song; it's no good.
2. No one's going to record this.
3. You don't belong here.
4. You can't talk to the president of a record company; he'll know you're just a small-town hick.

It's list time again! Get out your notebook.

We all have developed ideas about how we should act and how successful we should be. Until we change these ideas and make it okay to succeed, we will continue to sabotage our own efforts.

List 1: List ten reasons why you deserve a record or publishing deal, a job at a record company or whatever your end goal may be.

List 2: Write down three things you may be doing to avoid achievement. These could include: procrastination, poor planning, having no personal or professional goals, or refusing to apply yourself to your chosen profession.

Discuss these lists with a trusted friend or associate to give you a truthful "reality check." To succeed you will have to be able to separate yourself from your ego and to take tough criticism. Can you remember events in your life when you felt good, successful, fulfilled? How did you achieve these results? How were you conditioned to succeed? What resources did you rely on to achieve your goals?

Use your memory to recall the opposite; moments of inadequacy, fear or failure. What were your feelings at the time, and why? Many of our early childhood experiences determine our emotional reactions as adults. If we can use our memories to recall our experiences, then we can begin to understand why we react as we do. All of us were once children, and the inner child can often be accountable for our deepest feelings and fears.

1. Eliminate the negative people in your life.
2. Find reasons to feel good about yourself.
3. Visualize your success. Imagine yourself where you want to be — in the studio, onstage, behind a desk in a record company.
4. Remember that your small victories and accomplishments will add up. Make sure every single day you work you do something for your career.

5. Network with people you respect; observe the way they move, talk and act.

6. Remember that the most successful individuals have doubts, fears and struggles too.

Negative Speak

"The record business is run by a bunch of crooks." "A&R people wouldn't know a good song if it bit them on the butt." "My music isn't like that crap on the radio." "I don't write songs for twelve-year-old girls to buy at the mall. My music is for people who think."

At one time or another I've heard all of the above statements, and many more, that can be classified as negative speak. They're clichés which camouflage insecurity on the part of the speaker, and they are a form of self-sabotage.

We really do have the power to change the negative to positive, but first we must become aware of this power. Most intelligent readers will agree that positive thoughts bring positive results and negative thoughts bring negative results, but they have trouble making this concept work in their own lives and careers.

It's always easier to say something bad than to say something good. In writing this book I've had to identify my own negative thoughts and energies and concentrate on the positive. It would certainly be much easier for me to relate horror stories to you about the inner workings of the music industry, about deals I've seen go down, about the strangeness of the participants, but we can't concern ourselves with this; it's simple negativity.

We can't avoid negative thoughts and feelings; they're all too human. What we can do is try to find the lessons to be learned from all situations, to believe that we ultimately can succeed, to minimize setbacks while concentrating on the big picture, and to learn from our mistakes.

INVENTING AND REINVENTING YOUR PUBLIC PERSONA

In the entertainment world there is a certain type of personality that succeeds. Len Chandler, co-founding director of the Los Angeles Songwriters Showcase, former Columbia recording artist, and forty-year veteran of the music wars, emphasizes that one of the keys to success is "to be the type of person that other people want to help to succeed." This statement is blindingly clear. It's true that the farther up the ladder you go, the nicer people tend to be.

Music Biz Myth #5: *"In order to appear important you have to throw your weight around and immediately establish your verbal superiority."*

The Facts: It's often the smallest fish who tend to be the most obnoxious cretins and have the largest egos; in most cases their prime motivation is insecurity. To appear in your best light, be polite and gracious and considerate of others' feelings and abilities. Don't be tread on, but don't spread attitude around. Don't create a negative vibe around yourself. One of the first ways you're judged is by your personality and energy. Enthusiasm and positivity are qualities which attract others to you. Cultivate these traits to maximize your success.

Show business is made up of people who have successfully reinvented themselves. When Bob Dylan appeared in the early 1960s, he'd invented a new persona, name and history for himself, emulating his hero, Woody Guthrie. Madonna is a prime example of an entertainer who has successfully ascertained her audience's expectations, then exceeded them. Bruce Springsteen developed an audience by capitalizing on his "everyman" image; then transformed himself from an emaciated Jersey shore bar rat to a strapping, guitar-wielding rock and roll love god. Michael Jackson reinvented his face; George Michael transforms his image with each video in which he appears.

In show business your visual appearance is vital to your presentation. It's not enough to simply be good-looking (indeed, many of the heros of rock and roll music don't have this particular advantage) but a sense of style is a necessity. The best style is quite obviously the one which you alone have, but look for guidelines. Check out industry magazines for style tips, but be sure that the way you present yourself is not inappropriate and ludicrous. Also don't appear to be too obviously trendy; I'm sure we all blanch when we see old pictures of ourselves, but sometimes it's just the styles of clothing we're reacting to.

About Your Self-Image

Do you see yourself as a professional in the music business? Self-image is a barometer that you can manipulate any way you wish. You can see yourself in the sunlight or in the rain, and the way you perceive yourself is exactly the way you will be perceived by others, because positioning must first happen in your mind before it can happen in the minds of those with whom you meet and network.

Your physical appearance is strongly related to your self-image. A visual package based on the foundations of physical exercise, proper diet and good grooming techniques says to the people you meet that you care about yourself and what you do. In business, severely overweight people might be judged as out of control, very thin people as having eating disorders.

Excellent physical condition projects a good impression for several reasons. First, it indicates high self-esteem; a person who abuses his body is likely to have a poor opinion of himself. Second, it indicates discipline; for most of us it is no easy task to maintain a good physique. Third, it provides stamina and extra energy.

In the past decade, the image of the musician/producer as a drugged and alcohol-besotted individual has given way to one who is lean, trim and tough. Presidents of record companies lift weights and play racquetball. Executives in their late fifties project an attitude of youthful vigor, and rock stars can play four-hour shows without the aid of stimulants.

The above factors are controllable only by you; but you have to want to be in control. If you give up any element of control you're telegraphing signals that you don't like yourself.

And if you don't like yourself, don't expect others to.

How to Change What You Don't Like

First, define what is changeable and what is not. Hair color, eye color (via contact lenses) and muscle definition are all subject to change. If it's a physical transformation you desire, ask yourself why you feel you need to change. In managing talent I've observed that many times the best-looking individuals are the least secure about their looks. Instead of drastically changing your appearance, concentrate on the cultivation of a style that is uniquely your own.

There are professionals to help you do whatever you wish: hair stylists, weight trainers, people to determine what colors you should wear, etc. There are churches, hypnotherapists, psychologists, mediums and spiritualists to aid in your spiritual development. There are libraries, books, schools and classes to educate you.

The healthiest and most effective way to change anything about yourself is to change your attitude; learn to change all that you can, but also to accept the things about yourself that you can't change.

Your verbal skills are evaluated constantly in interacting with others. Do you hate the sound of your speaking voice on tape? Then practice sounding the way you think you should sound. According to legend, Demosthenes, the famous Greek orator of ancient times, practiced speaking above the roar of the ocean with a mouthful of pebbles to strengthen his verbal skills. Pretty extreme stuff, but the point is, any sound that can be made can be changed. On the telephone your verbal skills will determine whether or not you get through to the right people, so you need to sound confident, educated, articulate, relaxed and very polite. Working with a tape recorder and a qualified voice teacher can make your voice more effective. If you know you sound better, you'll be more likely to have a boost in self-esteem and confidence.

I received a call at the office this morning from a young lady who was in town from Canada and had been referred to me by a PR friend. She began our conversation by asking, "Is it true that the music business is all about who you know?" When I answered in the affirmative, her whiny tone became more pronounced. "I've been calling record companies and publishers and they say they don't accept unsolicited materials. I don't want to pay a music lawyer $900 an hour (I don't know a single one who charges that much!) to pitch my songs. What can I do?" At this point in the conversation I had to tell her the truth: I had turned off to her at the beginning of our conversation because of the negative tone in her voice, and the fact that she was soliciting "no" answers. I suspect that everyone she spoke with on the telephone had exactly the same reaction.

You will receive reflected positive responses from people you approach in an upbeat, positive manner. Your honest enthusiasm about a song, an opportunity, an act or an artist is something that can't be faked. Bluster and overhype are immediate turnoffs, but the energy generated by what you truly believe can be felt by others, and it can actually open doors for you that would otherwise be locked.

Show business is made up of self-centered people. An honest absorption in your project is to be expected, but never allow this to blind you to what other people are doing. When you encounter contacts in business or social life, it's absolutely imperative to find out what they're doing because:

1. Your interest in their project will be balanced by their interest in yours.

2. It makes them feel good that you care.

3. It gives them a chance to toot their own horn.

4. Most important, if they're doing something positive, there may be an opportunity for you to become involved.

An invaluable rule of human conduct is: Always make the other person feel important. To quote William James, "The deepest principle in human nature is the craving to be appreciated."

Remember the old adage "birds of a feather flock together"? Like many clichés, this one is painfully true. Friendship is vital to a productive life. Indeed, it's friendships that form your most vital network, so don't set yourself up for failure by hanging around with losers.

Losers are individuals whose negativity affects you adversely. They're quite often people who think of a thousand ways that something won't work; who have predetermined attitudes about people they don't know and places they haven't been. They know the music business is a corrupt game run by gangsters. They can always tell you what you did wrong in performance, why your song is not up to par, why the world is too ignorant to recognize their particular brand of genius. In business they're the people who are wasted in their present positions, aren't paid enough to be slogging through the mire that they're in, and should really be much farther up the ladder if there was any justice in this rotten world. These people are excess baggage and a waste of your time; cut them loose, now.

To be the type of person other people want to see succeed, first you have to project the image of a winner. Have a sense of humor, show your contacts that you have a human side and can discuss a variety of topics, not just yourself and your latest achievements. Show an honest interest in people and your shared reality in the world around you. Don't sell constantly, don't brag, don't run down other people; smile, give off a high-energy charm. Work on developing your conversational skills.

Since your network will be made up of people you consider friends, develop your friendship skills. Send cards and thank-you notes; let others know that you appreciate them and what they do for you.

What They See: Personal Appearance
In a music business office you'll usually see:

- Promotional T-shirts on many employees, male and female
- Denim jackets and jeans
- Earrings on men and women
- Current hairstyles
- Some retro hairstyles, including big hair on men
- Four-day beard growth
- Tattoos
- Sport coats thrown artlessly over the aforementioned T-shirts
- Hats
- Leather jackets and boots
- Van Dykes, goatees

Now imagine your young executive "dressed for success" in coat and tie walking into this environment. He'd immediately be judged as a "suit," an outsider. Coats and ties are OK, but use individuality in making your selections. A dress suit is only appropriate when dealing with lawyers or finance officers of record companies. This is good news for those of us without a lot of money, because style, fortunately, is free, and you can use a variety of outlets, including the old standby, the used clothing store, to have fun and create an identity for yourself. Visuals do more than make an immediate impression too—they also help make you memorable. It's not just your physical appearance but also your clothing that makes people remember you.

Try these devices:

- Lapel pins (good for starting conversations)
- Big men's sport coats (on women)
- A hat
- Bow-ties
- Ties in general
- A complete outfit from another decade
- Vintage shoes
- For women: something not normally used or thought of as a purse to carry your paraphernalia
- For men: a vintage, used briefcase
- Ethnic scarves

A coherent, recognizable style which is related to the music you create or represent is best. Cohesion is the obvious goal. One of the artists I currently manage can create a subtle impact simply by walking into a crowded restaurant in Hollywood. It's not because of overstatement; it's simply that his look is singular, natural and unique; he looks the part of a pop star. If you're a rap, rock, metal or reggae artist you have to look like one, but be sure to add your own personal touches to the "uniform," or you'll simply be imitating what others have done.

I attended a music business seminar where a young woman was complaining that she wasn't taken seriously in the music business and that men were always hitting on her in business situations. At the end of the class when she stood up to leave the room, I observed that she was wearing a shorter-than-short leather skirt, high heels and a see-through blouse. Her blond hair came from a bottle and her gait, no doubt affected by her spike-heeled shoes, was reminiscent of a lady of the night sashaying down Sunset Boulevard.

Women in the music business — a male-dominated arena where some of the men are prone to adolescent sexual behavior — have to be very careful what signals they're giving off when trying to be taken seriously as an artist or a businessperson. This is not to say that you need to dress puritanically, but since the area of male/female relations is tricky, don't add to the obstacles by sending out easily misinterpreted messages.

I had a phone call yesterday from a female singer/dancer who had been referred to me by her voice teacher. She knew we were auditioning backup singers for one of my clients and was eager to be involved. I told her that we had decided to use only male singers for the series of concerts, but because I was interested in what she was doing professionally, I asked her to send me a tape, résumé and bio (pretty standard stuff) to keep on file for upcoming opportunities. Her response floored me: "You producers are all alike," she said. "You just want to go out with me." Now keep in mind that (a) she'd never met me, (b) we were on the phone so I couldn't see her; she may well have resembled my Uncle Henry for all I knew.

I would never consider subjecting my acts, musicians or crew to someone who had such an attitude because music is a cooperative effort and requires the correct chemistry between many people. In a band or show situation, an incorrect attitude from one person can severely throw off the entire balance of the rest of the group.

I imagine that, unfortunately, the singer/dancer had a bad experience, and I can certainly sympathize with her; however, not all men in the music industry are pigs.

Men and women who rely on an overtly sexual physical presentation usually don't have much going for them in any other areas, or they are so insecure that they're forced to rely on attributes other than musical ones.

What to Wear Where!

When I first accepted the position as advertising director for the *Songwriters Musepaper*, I went out on sales calls dressed in a promotional rock and roll T-shirt with faded jeans, a leather jacket, a three-day growth of beard and an earring. I got the sales too. I was selling advertising space to small-scale recording studio owners, and, in my experience, this was how they dressed during daytime hours. By dressing like them, I gained their trust. Also, of course, I read all the technology magazines for studio owners, knew all of the latest equipment, and could recognize the outboard and recording gear on sight.

It's a pretty well-known sales trick that you have to look the part, and the more you can resemble the person you're selling to, the better your chances of closing the sale. This technique can backfire though, so you'll have to research your prospects. A good rule of thumb: When in doubt whether to dress up or down, dress up. It's better to appear a little classier than to be viewed as a bum. For entertainers the trick is to always dress like you're something special, because you are.

What to Wear to a Meeting

With a club owner. Club owners are indeed curious beasts. I have been fortunate to work for some of the best, and lucky enough to have avoided most of the worst. Keep in mind that the club owner has only one priority — to sell drinks. If you can help him do this, fine; if not, your career will be short-lived.

Mixed signals can work well for the musician/businessperson. Try crossing over conventional stage gear with a sport coat. Since you're playing two roles, you have to present both in your attire. For nice clubs, dress up, though again, define your show biz position by being just a little flashier, and let your appearance indicate that you can take charge, command attention, and conduct yourself like a professional.

With a lawyer or manager. Let their personal style dictate yours. Many managers are very casual, but music business lawyers are not—especially if they have offices with more conservative older partners. Some of the lawyers in Los Angeles dress much like rock and roll musicians it's true, but they're far outnumbered by the more conservative dressers. A lawyer is a vital part of your team in any music industry contractual dealings, and they generally work on the retainer system. You should look like someone who'll pay your bill on time and knows how to take care of business. A coat and tie for men is not inappropriate.

With managers it's a mixed bag. I've seen high-level managers in shorts and Hawaiian shirts, and I've seen them in Pierre Cardin suits. Managers are very much their own people and, theoretically, don't have to answer to anyone (except their artists). If you're an entertainer, though, look like an entertainer, but here in Los Angeles we have observed that it's the "wanna-be's" who overdress, not the heavy hitters.

Record company A&R people are usually out in the clubs till all hours. They're overworked, underpaid rock and roll survivors, and they look it. The hipness quotient is very high and most of the descriptions earlier in this chapter of record company apparel also apply to A&R and publicity personnel. If you're invited to meet label employees as an artist, show respect in your apparel, but don't be overdressed. A sport coat without a tie works fine.

At music industry conventions. As a producer of the Songwriters Expo, the world's largest educational and discovery event held for songwriters, I can always spot the amateurs and the out-of-towners. They're the ones who look uncomfortable in their clothes, are overdressed for ten hours of walking and sitting in classes and workshops, and attempt to look overly hip with flashy clothes and footwear incapable of traversing the halls and expansive distances of the convention center where the event is held.

At conventions a conversation piece is essential. You'll be meeting a lot of strangers, and having something for them to focus on gives them something to begin speaking to you about. People are basically shy and insecure in these settings and need a reason to speak with you. They may be dying to do so and the strange little tchotchke you have in your lapel may be the key.

In networking you need to speak with everyone, everywhere, all of the time. When you're in a setting where you have direct access to people who share your aspirations and interests, give yourself every opportunity to be approachable. P.S. Don't wear sunglasses indoors unless you're Yoko Ono or Ray Charles.

In a networking situation, honesty and a sense of humor are your most valuable tools. Many people are insecure, so it's up to you to dispel their insecurity by taking an active role in engaging them in conversation. You will never go wrong by beginning with an honest compliment. Look your contacts directly in the eyes, concentrate your energies on them, and be sure to smile. Ask general questions to keep them talking. For the period of time that you've engaged them, let them be your entire world.

Do:
- Ask, then remember, their name. Use it repeatedly in the conversation to burn it into your memory.
- Use open body language. Keep your arms uncrossed.
- Be unerringly polite.
- Ask them what they do and why they happen to be there.
- Ask them for their business card.
- Use the environment around you to give you mutual topics of conversation.
- Sense when the conversation is coming to a logical conclusion.
- Keep the door open for future discussions.
- Let them know that you enjoyed speaking with them.
- If applicable, let them know that you'll give them a call.

Don't:
- Begin with a negative comment, e.g., "Isn't this pâté awful?"
- Say, "Where do I know you from?"
- Give off a sexual vibe.
- Talk about yourself continually.
- Look over their shoulder and talk to people passing behind them (though it's OK to acknowledge others with a smile or wave).
- Forget their name.
- Eat large hunks of food while speaking.
- Say anything negative about any person present.
- Pressure them in any way.
- Act desperate.

Make Them Remember You

A strong handshake, a well-modulated voice, an air of confidence, high energy, positivity, honesty, a sense of humor and a unified visual appeal will make you memorable.

When meeting people for the second or third time, don't assume that they know who you are. They'll appreciate it if you remind them: "Hi John, I'm Dan. We met last month at the BMI awards dinner." Generally this receives a favorable response, providing you made a favorable impression.

Information about music industry personalities is fairly easy to come by if you know the right sources. If you were going to meet with an A&R executive, wouldn't it help to know (a) what type of music he likes; (b) who he's signed to his label in the past; and (c) his likes and dislikes? Making others feel important is always a good approach. I've had success by knowing not only an industry mover's most recent successes, but also some esoteric piece of information. In addition to the magazines and periodicals that you should read regularly, I would recommend that you train yourself to read the small print on cassette J-cards and CD insert booklets, because this is where the real truth often lies, in the arranging and production credits, in the thanks, and in the listing of the songwriters, publishers, studios, musicians and management. Often there are also addresses for management offices.

Collecting interviews with music industry execs is a way to access vital information. There is an L.A.-based magazine called *Music Connection* that provides an A&R profile in each issue of their biweekly publication. The information is invaluable for anyone in the business, particularly personal managers or artists hoping to be signed. Once a year the *Music Connection* compiles this information into a special issue. You can contact them at (213) 462-5772, or write to: Music Connection Magazine, 6640 Sunset Blvd., Hollywood, CA 90028.

For a career in the music business, it's crucial to take stock of your assets and your liabilities. Since you're hopefully in this life to improve as a person as well as a music businessperson, you have to be honest with yourself and keep improving. Visualize your success; surround yourself with hardworking, honest, productive, positive people, and it's closer than you think.

We know that a network of people will be involved in determining our success. In order to cultivate these people, impress them and influence them, we have to first meet them. Networking is far-reaching; through your contacts you will meet their contacts and so on. Someone with whom you carry on a seemingly insignificant conversation at a cocktail party may well prove to be your most valuable ally in the future. We really will never know the end results of our network until we've achieved success and can then see, with perfect hindsight, how we did it.

So you've got to work hard on being a good, fun, giving person. Talk to everyone, everywhere. Cultivate your people skills, because your charm and enthusiasm are invaluable tools of influence. No matter how talented you may be, if others don't enjoy being around you, working with you and being a part of your network, you will not succeed.

CHAPTER FIVE

SELLING YOUR STUFF

S ales are a fact of business life. Sales can be as simple as the process of exchanging money for a soda at the corner market, or as complex as creating multinational corporations to market records. In the popular music world, rock, R&B and country concerts are sponsored by companies who have determined, through market research, that the audiences for these types of music are also the primary buyers of their products. We see music and sports stars pitching soda pop and lending their names to lines of shoes and clothing.

The skills that you develop in sales, and your comprehension of how necessary these skills are, can help you achieve success. In the music business you will be selling yourself and the music you represent to:

- Other performers/musicians
- Record companies
- Audiences
- Publishers
- Club owners
- Promoters
- Managers
- Agents

In this chapter you will learn how to call attention to, and how to sell, yourself. We will explore ways to give your project wings via the creation of a "scene" and learn how to convince the media to cover it. We'll look at examples of press releases and bios that have proven to be interesting enough to be included in major magazines and newspapers. Using your current skills and abilities, you can also discover how to barter creatively to save yourself thousands of dollars while widening your network and advancing your career.

SELLING YOURSELF FROM YOUR HOMETOWN

It used to be that bands and musicians had to move to New York, Nashville or Los Angeles to become successful. Not anymore. Even though these three cities continue to be the recording and media capitols, there is a strong regional backbone to success in the music business. The last couple of years have focused attention on such unlikely places as Athens, Georgia; Akron, Ohio; Minneapolis and Seattle.

Record companies like to see strong economics on a local or regional level, and your chances of signing a $1,000,000 contract with Warner Brothers are much greater if you can sell 10,000 copies of your cassettes and CDs regionally while performing in your local area. Believe me, if you can accomplish this feat someone will be dying to speak with you.

There are many levels of success in the music business. You can be successful locally, regionally, nationally or internationally.

Let's assume though that national and international recognition are the ultimate prizes. Here's one possible scenario: Your band meets in your hometown and begins playing local schools, teen clubs and events. Using a local recording studio (maybe on a partial "speculation deal" in which a studio owner gives you free studio time in exchange for a piece of your publishing action or a percentage of your signing advance when you are paid to sign a contract with a major record label), you record cassettes or CDs for distribution at your gigs, use the money from the sales to create T-shirts, and use the funds accrued from both of the above to make a video. In the meantime, the local radio station becomes involved and begins to sponsor regional appearances for your band as well as playing your songs on the air. With the video you can use local television outlets and generate sponsorship interest with local businesses in your region.

Your band continues to broaden its performance base, venturing farther and farther from your hometown. You use your extensive audience to generate a database to promote upcoming shows and new products. All of your cassettes, CDs and merchandise come with "bounceback" materials, so your buyers can order more and varied forms of merchandise. Your band also creates a newsletter to announce upcoming shows and to advertise new products. You involve sponsors on local, regional and national levels who have a desire to be visible to the particular demographic group (which you can identify through market research; questions you ask in your newsletter about their buying habits).

Management would be very attracted by the initiative shown by your band; so would a record label. Since your group has already proven itself, you will be much less of a risk to a record company who could conceivably invest hundreds of thousands of dollars in your success. You also will have proven that there is a market for what you're doing and that you are aggressive and resourceful enough to go for it.

Don't rule out local opportunities. Million-selling group Color Me Badd made it a point to hang out in the hotel lobby in Kansas City where the big touring bands stayed when they'd perform at the local amphitheater. They met their producer this way. Local contacts are essential; include the following in your list of people to meet, cultivate and make aware of what you're doing:

1. **Local media, print and electronic.** Local radio stations often have shows featuring local talent and produce events which you could use to give your act credibility and visibility. Local newspapers, magazines and freebies can also make you more visible and give you the all-important "clips" for your press kit. Keep in mind that in order to entice the media you need a strong focused visual package, great pictures (particularly action shots), bios, logos and a cover letter, which will make the media more interested in giving you space in their publications.

It is also much easier to gain press if you're doing something newsworthy. Performing for local charities is a wonderful source of exposure for budding acts; local video shows are bursting out all over and need local celebrities with video product.

2. **Concerts and clubs.** Performing as an opening act for touring groups is a proven method of advancing your career. The band's management, agents and contacts can be valuable. Performing in clubs can be a good starting point for a career, but if your ultimate goal is to be a concert act you can never start early enough. Fairs, street festivals and carnivals can have the big-time concert atmosphere, plus a large built-in audience. If you can convince organizers to let you play, even for free, you can cover your expenses by selling T-shirts or cassette tapes. You can also use these particular opportunities to create your mailing list, by having sign-up sheets filled out by audience members.

3. **Recording studios.** What a great place to meet music people. There's an art to hanging out in the studios though. The main thing is to keep out of the way, keep your mouth shut, don't put anything on the console (ever!!!), and be supportive. Also, don't give your advice unless you're asked. The best way to be in the studio is if you're wanted, needed or working there, and interning has a long and time-honored tradition of opening doors. Songwriter Kris Kristofferson was a janitor at RCA in Nashville; that's how he made many of his contacts. Do everything in your power to be around the studio environment; it's the best place to learn about music as a recorded medium.

4. **Video facilities** are a close second to recording studios for meeting musicians, managers, players and bands. Again, if you can work there, even for free, take the opportunity. There's a whole set of equipment and a language you'll need to master. See it firsthand. There is always a place for someone to help out at the shoot.

5. **Personal relationships** are the key to successful networking. Cultivate every opportunity to meet people. Be sincere, be honest, be the kind of person they want to meet. Other musicians and songwriters can provide not only obvious economic opportunities, but also a much-needed emotional support system.

Start Your Own Organization

If you want to be a part of a music industry group and don't have one in your area, maybe you should take the initiative and start one. What you need is a common focus, ways of finding and contacting potential members, a place to hold your initial get-togethers, a theme, a name, and you're off.

I just returned from the desert community of Palm Springs where I was invited, along with assorted record company personnel and music publishers, to speak to an organization that was just forming. Not a previously known hotbed of musical action (unless you count the late Liberace), the community is close enough to Los Angeles to allow residents the opportunity to visit there often. A diverse group of writers came out to present strong, consistent material. The hook to this event was that by bringing in publishers to evaluate the songs and pick them up for possible signings, there was an immediate focus, and possible reward. The sponsoring organization brought in a local radio station to act as a sponsor, committed their community newspaper to donate ad space, and a leading local hotel to put us all up free. The event was very rewarding for all of the participants, but best of all, the Palm Springs locals have succeeded in founding an organization, and they now are able to network among themselves.

If you want to start a networking organization you have an obvious reason to contact executives in the music business, and you can work your own personal agenda into that of the organization. You can use the greater power of the group to promote events focusing on your music or bands with which you're involved. You can use your invitations and overtures to key players in the music industry to form the relationships so vital to success in the business. You can make your name known and your influence felt much more effectively with the power of an organization behind.

Creating a Scene

Virtually every important trend in pop music has come out of a "scene." From Liverpool and San Francisco in the 1960s, to New York punk in the 1970s, Minneapolis in the 1980s, and Seattle and Athens, Georgia, in the 1990s, music has been tied together with fashion, locale, and a certain and specific sense of time and place.

Having a scene or being a part of one has many advantages. The first of course is that it provides a network of people to work with. The press is attracted to a scene because it gives them a handle, something they can name, and an opportunity to write about the influences, personalities, sociology and fashion of what's around the music. Audiences of course are attracted to a scene because it gives them an opportunity to become a part of what they deem is "happening." Record companies are attracted to bands that come out of scenes because they recognize there is interest in what's being created; hence, there's a buying populace and momentum which, if marketed correctly, could trigger a national phenomenon.

Eight Necessary Ingredients to the Creation of a Scene

1. An open-minded progressive audience (preferably college age or younger)
2. Enough bands to sustain interest
3. Supportive press, preferably nonmainstream
4. Venues in which to present artists
5. A specific sense of style and fashion singular to the music
6. Graphic artists and photographers to capture the picture

7. Visionaries and high-energy leaders
8. A sense of community among creative people

If you can't identify or be a part of a pre-existing scene, I would strongly suggest that you band together with others to create your own. The way to achieve this begins with your thinking of the big picture, not just your next week's gig. Target your act to a group of buyers; send regular press releases and newsletters to mailing lists; display flyers and posters at locales where your strongest audience is found. T-shirts, caps, buttons and bumper stickers turn the wearers into walking billboards for your act. Ads in local papers and music magazines or on radio and television can often be obtained free if you bring the media in as a co-sponsor of your events. In the creation of a scene, you have to be event-oriented rather than just going from week to week and performing for a limited audience.

It is helpful to have hangout locations where scene members can gather and exchange ideas. When I recently interviewed record producer Roger Bechirian (who has produced Squeeze, Elvis Costello and Nick Lowe), he shared his memories of London in the mid-seventies, when the Sex Pistols were shaking up the world of rock and roll. The physical center of that scene happened to be the London leatherwear shop of the Pistols' manager. Many times these centralized locales are the clubs where the bands play, record stores, or even the office of the magazines that write about them.

I was in New York City in 1975 when the punk movement exploded out of CBGB's, a tiny, smelly bar on the Bowery. Groups like Television, The Talking Heads, Blondie and The Ramones played there every night. There was a strong sense of community among the bands, a common language of alienation and urban chaos, and the scene gained national recognition in a short time.

Form a community with your local musicians: share information, music, experiences, rehearsal halls and gigs. When Jane's Addiction leader Perry Farrell formed the first Lollapallooza Tour, he brought rock, metal, alternative and rap artists together in a phenomenal show which, in two consecutive summers, was the biggest event going. Even though the audiences for these bands were diverse, the bands were all working outside the commercial mainstream, had strong messages and a political orientation. By involving local organizations and giving political and environmental groups booths, the tour achieved a grander scale and affected audiences emotionally, musically and politically, and made a big heap o'money to boot.

Although you may not have national bands as your contacts, you can use this approach locally. Look for common threads with other bands, musicians, writers and audiences; exploit these connections and make the sum total bigger than the individual elements. Everyone wins.

COMING IN SIDEWAYS

One of the realities of being in a music capitol is that it's hard to earn money performing. If you're used to working in clubs to earn a living wage in your hometown, you'll be shocked when your band is asked to pay $900 to perform in some sleazy club in New York or L.A. It's simply a matter of supply and demand; if supply is up, demand is down. In a city where there are literally thousands of musicians fighting for visibility, there are few opportunities to earn money playing in clubs. The $100 per night per player or so you might make in Cleveland, Ohio, as a working musician is nonexistent in the big city. Consequently, if you're moving to a major music center, unless you're financially independent, you may need to get a day job.

The best type of day job for music people is one which doesn't require a lot of your time or creativity, is flexible, and calls for a negligible commitment on your part. Waiter and waitress gigs are perfect for this (here in L.A. we talk about the quintessential "actor/ singer/model/dancer/waiter"). When I first came to Los Angeles, I worked in a phone sales position. Not high on the prestige ladder to be sure, but I made enough to survive, worked only mornings, and no one was even aware I was working a straight job, since I didn't schedule any music sessions until I got off work at noon; it was just assumed that I was a night owl. Best of all, most of the other people working there were also music business people, and we could network and exchange information to help each other out.

Working the same unholy sales job (which was actually selling after-dinner mints to Ma 'n' Pa stores and restaurants. EEK!) was a girl singer I recognized from her nightly appearances on a syndicated television game show. When I inquired why she was working such a lowly job, she explained that it took two weeks out of the year to shoot all of the season's episodes. She still had fifty weeks left to work. So much for the glamour of television.

Working in the Business

Other hopefuls aspire to jobs in the business itself. The mail room is the starting place for many people (including David Geffen, who began his legendary career at the William Morris agency) and is still a way in. Many record companies have adopted a new policy, however, and won't hire songwriters or performers to work in their offices. Nowadays, jobs in the mail room at the Morris Agency require a college degree. Also, some major music companies refuse to listen to submissions from their employees.

On the local or regional level, record store jobs can offer valuable music business experience. You can meet promo people from the various labels, come into contact with marketing companies, and see firsthand what type of promotion and product will make buyers walk away with the latest CD clutched in their eager hands.

Radio stations are also good break-in points to observe how this end of the business works, to find out what records get played, and why. Working for a local concert promoter may offer valuable contacts for future endeavors, as well as educating you about the realities of the touring business.

The touring business itself is the modern equivalent of running away with the circus; it's hectic, it's crazy, the money is bad, the coffee worse and the hours intolerable. But for someone aspiring to the management or production end of the business, it's an education to go out on a concert tour as a roadie or a technical person.

The Business of the Business

There's the record business, which is the recording, sale and manufacturing of records, and there's the music business, which includes everything else. Here in Los Angeles we see hundreds of cottage industries which are satellites to the music business. Recording and demo studios help performers and writers put their materials into listenable/salable form. Producers, arrangers and musicians are available to help with the process. Photographers and video technicians document the music visually. Clothing experts, hair stylists, photographers and image consultants will work with labels and artists in creating a strong visual presentation. Public relations consultants and bio writers work with the bands, press agents and publicists helping them promote their gigs. Artists and musicians can study with vocal instructors and live performance consultants in classroom and studio situations. Journalists document the scene, and thousands of people make their living off of the needs of the aspirant.

In your local market, consider niche marketing: establishing yourself to do what no one else is doing, as a way to make a viable career in music. I've seen it work for many people in the music capitals who had the foresight and imagination to create their own role. People become important because they act important. Niche marketing and cottage industries are a way to meet talent and to get in on the ground floor of their developing careers.

Journalism

If you can write, you may be someone whom the music business not only accepts, but actually needs. Jon Landau, Bruce Springsteen's manager, began his career with the Boss as a journalist, reviewing Bruce's performances. Writing about acts for your local rock rag immediately puts you in the flow of things, in touch with breaking trends in the music business as well as the publicity departments of the record labels, artist management and the acts themselves. It can also give you local notoriety and access to all sorts of entertainment, information, record release parties and people. You'll actually be invited to many affairs, and have opportunities to move into other sectors via the written word.

Start by contacting your local music and entertainment publications to determine their policies on working with freelancers. Be observant of the editorial styles of the publication to which you're submitting and what you may be able to add journalistically to reinforce the magazine's viewpoint. Also, take note of what may be missing from a magazine that you can write about. I became the world music editor of an L.A.-based music magazine simply by observing that no one was writing about the vibrant global forms. It was as easy as calling and submitting an article.

Once you begin freelancing for one magazine, you'll have "clips" or copies of your articles to audition your abilities for others. The more publications you can write for, the more extensive your influence. If you believe in your ability to write, don't be afraid to do it on spec (they buy the piece after you've written it, *if* they like it).

Many music writers begin to play the other side of the fence; since they understand how the press works, they can begin to do public relations and provide publicity services for acts they may meet. Although it is frowned upon (as well as unethical) to write articles about acts you represent, if you write for local publications, odds are you'll meet up with other writers you can include in your network who will offer the journalistic support that you, because of potential conflict of interest, are unable to provide. They may have the same needs also.

Magazines are ultimately ruled by advertising dollars. Articles which can reinforce the positions of their strongest advertisers are always welcome, and any article which makes the magazine more appealing to a wider group of buyers will certainly be of interest, because this information can help convince advertisers to gamble precious advertising dollars to reach consumers.

Another quick way into the publication world is by selling advertising space. This is generally a commission job, but if you need valuable hours to work on music projects, are self-motivated, disciplined and aggressive, this is a way to make money while being part of the big picture.

For aspiring recording artists in particular, it's probably better not to announce to everyone how you make a living; be subtly enigmatic, because what people imagine you do for money is probably much more interesting than the truth anyway.

If you're a future mogul working at a straight job, be sure to be able to access your incoming phone calls and messages, to give the appearance that you're running a full-time management or production company even if you're slaving away for someone else. An answering service is a businesslike alternative.

Music Biz Myth #6: *If I can work full time, I can make more money; then I can invest this money in my career.*

The Facts: Don't make too much money at your straight gig. When I first went to New York, I naively asked someone, "What happens to all the people who come here to be successful and aren't?" He informed me that many of them took straight jobs to pay the rent, became discouraged at their lack of progress in show business and, as they kept moving up in their straight job, learned to like the lifestyle that more money could give them. They eventually blended into the populace at large.

If you do what you do in the hope of accruing vast sums of money, please don't go into the music business; there are easier ways to afford a BMW.

We all have limited energies and creativity; if we expend them on behalf of someone else's business we're short-changing ourselves. Sure it's possible to work at any number of things and make enough money to have a comfortable lifestyle, but if you want success in the music business (which ultimately will pay off in emotional satisfaction as well as monetary gain), you can't give up your vision and creativity. Guard them jealously, and use them to fuel your ambitions.

BARTERING

As of this writing, I am executive producing a video which is being edited at Sony Pictures in L.A. It's on a soundstage using equipment that costs more than the annual budgets of many emerging nations. Know how much we're paying for the facility? Nothing, it's free. How can this be?

Recording studios and engineers need products to demonstrate what they do. An artist on the move can demonstrate equipment and facilities to great advantage for technicians. Songwriters need demos of their songs, singers need tapes of their voices in the studio. These are perfect opportunities to marry two needs so "everybody wins." The reason we're at Sony is that someone who works on a network TV show has started a film company and needs video products to show off his abilities. I happen to manage an artist who needs a dynamite video, so it's a match that works.

Photographers can always use a visually interesting person for their portfolio, so often it's possible to get 8 × 10s for just the price of the film and developing. In order to effectively barter, the persons involved must not only need each other, but must be equally qualified.

Many successful musicians are great barterers. I've seen the "You play on my demo and I'll play on yours" trick done to great advantage. There are also rock bands who will roadie for their friend's band at special gigs. No band wants to be seen schlepping their equipment onstage, so their musician friends set up for them in exchange for their doing the same for their friend's band.

I have a client who is both a vocalist and vocal instructor. Whenever he performs at showcase clubs in Los Angeles, his band features many of the hottest players in town. For their participation in his show, he gives them vocal lessons. Of course he has to use players who need vocal lessons (you can't barter with something that the other party doesn't need), but he's been very successful at using players who can use his services too.

When I lived in New York, I hooked up with an audio engineering school that needed guinea pigs so their students could learn how to record and mix music in the studio. Since my band always needed development time and great demos, we were able to work with students who were learning their chops at the same time that we were learning about arranging and recording in major facilities. In this way we got 24-track demos of our stuff to shop at will.

Many recording studios will hire "second" engineers to work for very little money. In order to keep these people working, they will give them free access to "down" time, or time which isn't booked, to work on their own projects. Since most recording engineers aspire to produce, if you can hook up with someone in this position you can work together to achieve common goals.

Because many of your contacts are also searching for outlets for their own creativity, to make bartering work, you only need to meet enough ambitious people to form your network of contacts. It's your job to create the energy and momentum around your projects, to be able to sell the vision to potential collaborators and investors, and to create a vehicle which others want to climb onto because it looks like it's going somewhere.

We all have individual paths to walk in our achievement of success, if we can walk that road with others it makes the way much less lonely.

Talents/Services to Barter Within Your Network
- Computer skills
- Telephone/telemarketing ability
- Public relations
- Carpentry (I know a musician who helped build a recording studio in exchange for studio time for his own projects. He was also allowed to sell time to his contacts at a discount.)
- Teaching music or voice
- Electrical work/wiring
- MIDI/programming
- Child care
- Foreign language proficiency

- Teaching dance/choreography
- Graphic design/art
- Photography/darkroom skills
- Makeup/hair design
- Truck transportation
- Writing skills
- Gardening
- Catering/cooking
- Pet care
- Instrument repair
- Furniture refinishing

I have compiled this list from talking with real people about their experiences; these talents and services were bartered for recording and video editing time, voice lessons and the services of technicians and musicians. But bartering requires creativity, not only in evaluating what you have to barter, but also in knowing how to approach contacts within your network who may require your services — in a word, salesmanship — a topic we'll cover later in this chapter.

A WORD ABOUT MONEY

Of course you can't barter for everything. At some point you will need to put money into your career to realize a return. Whether that money is your own or someone else's depends on several factors, including the extent of your own personal resources and how successful you are in getting investors excited about your career. No one will invest in your career if you haven't bothered to do so yourself. Networking is the best way to assure that your money is being well spent, that you're using creative bartering to offset many of your expenses, and that your project has gained enough momentum so that others want to ride the magic bandwagon. The truth is, it's necessary to put out, to cast your bread upon the waters, to impress, and particularly, to launch an act.

Just as no magic person will fly from the woodwork to help you make a career, so no magic person will give you money without some serious terms behind it. Outside investors can be very expensive. In a business as speculative as the music business, there is obviously a greater chance for failure than for having money returned or a profit made. I've seen family and friends become involved in artists' careers, and I've seen hard feelings, emotional upset, and distrust evolve because of mishandled and badly accounted funds.

If you are planning to ask any of your networking contacts for funds, be as professional as possible in putting together a business-like proposal. You'll have a much better chance of raising money for your project if:

- You have a track record of success.
- You have a clear-cut business plan.
- The funds are for a specific endeavor, e.g., a video or a 24-track master to subsidize a concert tour, not just overall funds.
- You can establish a payback plan.

In your own best interests, have a cap on the repayment of any investment funds from outside investors. For example if an investor gives you $10,000 and you agree to pay him 20 percent of your earnings over a year's time, you could end up repaying much, much more than his initial investment plus interest. Limit his percentage of your future earnings.

The more of your earnings you can retain control of, the healthier and wealthier you'll be in the long run. I've seen acts go into their first record deal owing so much money (not to mention the recoup-ables that the record company advances them) that they would have to sell back-to-back platinum records before seeing a single penny in profit.

Ultimately, the best money to invest in your project is your own. If you want to make millions in the music business, how much money are you willing to invest to make that happen? And if you won't invest in your own career, don't expect others to.

Do Not Hand Your Money Over for the Following:

- Songsharks—those who ask you to pay to have your songs recorded for release. These folks work the copyright lists in Washington, D.C., to find names, and then invite you to send your songs for review. If you do, you will then receive a congratulatory letter announcing your inclusion on their upcoming album, and they will ask you for money. Don't send it; tear up their letters immediately. These companies have nothing to do with the legitimate music business.
- Lists of agents and managers.
- Home addresses of stars.
- Having your song played on the radio.

• Having your band included on a compilation album unless you know the company, their history, and their outlets for the record. There are good compilations, and there are bad ones.

• Appearing on a television program (particularly public access).

• Performing in a club, although bands may be asked to pre-sell tickets.

• A music business "consultant" who claims to be able to use his contacts to get your tape in the proverbial "right hands." There is an unscrupulous operator in Los Angeles who typically bilks unsuspecting bands out of $8,000 at a time. What he does is not technically illegal, so he continues to prosper. Often his victims are so ashamed that they won't tell anyone about their experience or instigate legal action, so this bottom-feeding sleaze is still operating.

If you ever have a question about specific ethics in a business practice, don't be intimidated. A good resource to contact is the Los Angeles Songwriters Showcase who are hip to most of the scams being perpetrated on the unwary by shady operators. Call LASS at (213) 467-7823 if you feel you're being asked to pay money for a hustle. Sleaze merchants prey on the uneducated and those with stars in their eyes. Be pragmatic and know the business; you'll be much safer.

Do Invest Wisely in the Following:
• Publicity and public relations services.

• Quality recordings. (But keep this in perspective; you don't need 24-track song demos to play for publishers.)

• Equipment.

• Costumes.

• Photos and graphic services.

• Business cards.

• A fax/answering machine.

• A computer. (Macintosh has wonderful design capabilities in addition to sequencing software and interface for multi-track recording plus data management for Rolodex/mailing lists.)

• Musicians. Marta Woodhull, in her ground-breaking book, *Singing for a Living* (Writer's Digest Books), suggests reasons to always pay musicians for their efforts, even if it's not a great deal of money. One reason is that it keeps your dealings on a professional level; if someone is doing you a favor, playing for free, and they happen to be a half hour late for a rehearsal, it's very difficult to give them a hard time for their tardiness. On the other hand, if you're paying them money out of your pocket, even a small amount, you have the necessary leverage to demand a certain degree of professionalism.

- Quality tape duping, mastering and labeling.

SALESMANSHIP 101

As consumers we're being sold to constantly; every hour of radio listening, television watching and newspaper and magazine reading involves sifting through the various buying opportunities we encounter. If you create a product or a service, it's essential to know a few basics about how the buying mentality really works.

- For the most part, all buyers purchase for these two emotional reasons: pride of ownership and prestige. They want to buy.
- Know exactly who your buyer is and what his needs are. If you're booking an act into a local club for instance, you know that the bottom line is this: the club owner wants to sell drinks. Show that you can help him achieve this by attracting an audience. Provide recommendations, letters of reference and referrals. If this doesn't work and you know you can pack the club, try this: Offer to perform one night in his venue for free. If you can't do what you promise, he doesn't have to pay you. Have him agree to hire you for a couple of weeks if you deliver.
- Know your product inside and out. Product knowledge gives you confidence, and confidence helps you make the sale.
- Don't be afraid to close the sale. If you're trying to give someone a buying opportunity for your services or the services of the act you represent, give them multiple opportunities to say yes. There are as many closes as there are sales approaches, but always try for an affirmative response and don't give your buyer too many options. "Would you like us to perform next week, or would the week after be better for you?" is a better close for a club owner than "Would you like us to play here?"
- No doesn't always mean no — generally it's only an objection. For every objection there is an appropriate response. Rehearse the sales scenario in your mind and anticipate any objection your buyer may have; answer his objection directly and go back to the close.
- Successful sales presentations have limited time frames. As

buyers we're used to seeing things like "limited time only" special sales. This is a very common device to force a buying decision or close. "I want to think about it" from a buyer is not a good sign and diminishes the probability that he will ever buy. Since buyers buy for emotional reasons, keep the energy level high, and make it look like any decision has to be made at the moment it's presented.

• A good salesman assumes the sale; it is a foregone conclusion. What you're selling is right for the buyer isn't it? Otherwise, why are you trying to sell him something he doesn't need or want?

The Steak and the Sizzle

It's a well-known sales technique that if the buyer buys the credibility of the salesperson he will generally buy the product the salesman is presenting. Selling doesn't have to be a sleazy, deceptive proposition. It's actually a valuable service.

Although there is a certain aggressive and charismatic personality type who is referred to as a "born salesman," almost anyone can succeed by understanding the basics. It's essential to be a good listener, because no one likes to be talked at, so actively engage any buyer through dialogue. Open-ended questions like "What type of entertainment do you envision for your event," and close-ended questions, such as "Do you want blues, reggae or rock and roll," help qualify your buyers so you're not wasting your time or theirs.

Never be intimidated by your buyers. Your time is just as important as theirs, so don't sit interminably in their office, allow them to browbeat you, or cast yourself as overly appreciative for the appointment. Don't attempt to butter up buyers, and don't beat around the bush; get to the point. Always begin by telling the buyer what you're going to sell him. He'll appreciate your honesty, and honesty helps win sales.

REFERRALS

Referrals are the best way to approach someone you don't know. If you can use the name of someone your new contact knows and respects, you'll increase your odds of speaking with him. Never be afraid to ask someone for a referral if you think he'll give you one. However, if you're pitching materials or songs, make sure your contact feels strongly about what you have; otherwise, you're putting him in an awkward position by asking for his help.

Sometimes this approach works: "I'll send it to you to hear, and if you like it, I'd appreciate a referral to Mr. Jones at Acme Records. I know how important your integrity is, and I wouldn't want to put you in a tough position. OK?"

Now suppose you need to reach someone and don't have a referral, but think your odds would be better if you mentioned the name of a person they would instantly recognize; should you lie just to get through to them?

I would never advise anyone to be less than honest; however, I admit that I did try this on at least one occasion, and it didn't help; I still didn't get through. In the sales game many things can unconsciously give you away if you're not being honest. If you have the goods, you'll get referrals. However, a telephone is not a court of law; you're in business to make money too. Let your own sense of morals justify your actions. Don't use my name though!

TELEPHONE TRICKS FOR THE TIMID

The telephone is the single most powerful communication tool ever developed. Just as a musician must develop his skills in playing an instrument, so you must treat the telephone like an instrument, and develop your selling skills accordingly. Here's how to put the telephone to work for you.

It is absolutely necessary to script what you're going to say before you make a call. Your script doesn't have to be word-for-word, but it does have to be outlined. You may have ten seconds to make a favorable impression — don't blow it by improvising.

Theodore Roosevelt is credited with coining a term "weasel word." They are "words that destroy the force of a statement by equivocal qualification as a weasel ruins an egg by sucking out its content while leaving it superficially intact." *Might, maybe* and *perhaps* fall into this category. So do phrases such as "I just happened to," "I was wondering if," "I think you ought to," and "Sorry to bother you, but . . . ." These terms instantly show your self-doubt and telegraph your insecurity.

You should always have visual contact with a mirror when you're doing any heavy-duty phone calling. Did you know that a smile can be heard on the telephone? Try it sometime when you're talking to a friend. Don't talk *at* people, be responsive to them and learn to listen to what they're saying to you. Receptionists and secretaries can be your allies; learn their names, don't expect them to educate you, and treat them well.

Sometimes when it's extremely hard to get through to an executive, try calling earlier than the office opens, or about a half hour after it closes. Many times the support staff leaves, so the exec has to answer his own phone.

Please only use this next approach if you believe you're totally on target, because it can be abrasive. You'll need to rehearse this one. We're calling William Jones. We absolutely believe that what we have to say will interest him, but he's hard to get through to. This is the approach:

Receptionist: Acme Records.

Me: William Jones, please.

Receptionist: Who shall I say is calling?

Me: Dan Kimpel. May I speak with William Jones, please?

Receptionist: What company are you with?

Me: DKM Management. Would you put me through to William Jones, please?

Receptionist: Will he know what this is regarding?

Me: It's regarding a management client. Will you put me through to William Jones, please?

The point of this approach is not to harass an overworked receptionist; indeed, keep your tone friendly but very strong. It's a rare receptionist who won't back down after being asked, four times, to put you through. You've got to sound authoritative enough to convince her that you know Mr. Jones though, and that what you have to say is important to him.

Often if your phone presence is strong enough you won't have to go through all of this, but it's usually not necessary to tell your whole tale unless you're asked to.

This is generally a more typical scenario:

Receptionist: Acme Publishing, good morning.

Me: Good morning, this is Dan Kimpel from DKM Management. May I speak with William Jones, please?

Mr. Jones: William Jones.

Me: Good morning, Mr. Jones. This is Dan Kimpel from DKM Management. I'm calling on behalf of a client who has some very strong, accessible R&B material. I know the recent successes your company has had, your role in signing that material, and I'd like to set up a brief appointment to play you three songs this week. Could we meet on Wednesday or Thursday?

At this point Mr. Jones may grill me further.

Mr. Jones: What type of songs are they?

Me: There's one strong, uptempo dance song (reader's tip: publishers always need uptempo stuff), a hip-hop midtempo funk tune and a power ballad. We have strong demos and the publishing is available. Could I come by for a face-to-face this week?

Mr. Jones: Sure, let me give you back to my secretary, and she'll schedule you in.

LEARN THE LANGUAGE

Nothing gives an amateur away like misuse of music business terms. I've heard some dillies: writers who have recorded demos and pronounce this "deemos." "Where do I sell my songs?" is a dead giveaway, because professionals don't "sell" songs; they have them signed, published, or cut, but not sold. "I need an agent or a manager" is another dead giveaway; these are totally separate functions. To learn the language of music it's essential to hang around with the people who speak it.

Musicians

To the uninitiated, the arcane language of professional musicians can sound like a foreign tongue, punctuated by the word "man" at least once per sentence. There is a musician-speak which could actually be the subject of a whole other book. Musicians generally like to talk about their gear — equipment that is. Learning about the various instruments and having strong opinions about them is a good opener; talk vintage guitars and you can't lose. Keyboard players tend to be tech heads, so know enough about the cutting-edge developments to sound knowledgeable. Never be afraid to ask a musician his opinion about instruments, or music for that matter; odds are they'll love to tell you.

Musicians can be very standoffish and insular. I've seen them be brutal to singers in a studio situation who didn't know how to ask for what they wanted. Some rudimentary music courses can be very helpful in communicating with musicians who may be in your network or employ.

Songwriters

You'll need to be conversant about the parts of a song. Know what a verse, bridge and chorus are. Know rhyme scheme terminology like AABB, ABAB. Know that songs are written, not "made up." Know about the demos and enough about the technology to get what you want in the studio. Know the terminology of the publishing business, what a "hold" is, what a co-publishing deal is, what actually happens when a publisher likes your song.

The book I mentioned earlier, *The Craft and Business of Songwriting*, by John Braheny, is a great place to begin to learn the songwriting language. Becoming affiliated with a local or national songwriter organization will put you in contact with other songwriters. Invest in a subscription to the *Songwriters Musepaper*, *American Songwriter Magazine* or *Songtalk*.

Within the Business

Know what a record deal, a spec deal, a publishing deal, points and recording fund are. Know enough musician-speak to be able to communicate, the same with recording studio jargon. You should begin learning about recording consoles, tape machines and outboard equipment. The best way to learn is by asking questions of those around you who know. Engineers and producers are generally very enthusiastic about discussing equipment.

When I interviewed Donald Passman in chapter three of this book, I was sitting in his office after a session talking about my management business. I told him I had taken courses at UCLA when I started in the business because I didn't know everything I thought I should know. Donald replied that, when you get into a new endeavor in the music business, it's not necessary to know everything off the bat; indeed, it's not necessarily an advantage. How you learn what you know through your experiences, and how you ultimately use this knowledge to become more effective is much more important.

Learning the language will become second nature to you. Be a sponge; read every book and periodical that you can about the business; attend seminars, classes and training sessions. But most of all, be around people who are doing what you want to do; the language will become instinctive and natural.

Hooples

When I lived in New York City I performed regularly at a night-club on Bleecker Street called the Back Fence. A Greenwich Village institution, the joint was run by two crusty brothers named Ernie and Rocky Scinto who spoke an intriguing and exotic New Yorkese which included the word "hoople." The first time I heard them use this word and asked what it meant, they looked at me as only New Yorkers can and replied, "Just what it sounds like." In the music business, hooples are people who call you up and, at the expense of your time, expect you to accommodate, facilitate and educate them. They don't know the first thing about the business or how it works. These people are time wasters.

Today a co-worker encountered a person on the elevator and brought him to meet me as a joke. This person was making the rounds of the music business buildings in Hollywood attempting to "sell" a smutty, misogynistic song that he'd recorded on cassette. He wanted to play it for me while I was on three phone calls and way too busy for such silliness. This man was a hoople.

Hooples are instantly indentifiable; don't be one.

Do This on the Phone:
- Script your call.
- Be honest.
- Get right to the point.
- Sound friendly.
- Use the name of the person you're speaking to at least once a minute.
- Be very courteous.
- Have a lot of energy!
- Sound intelligent.
- Turn off the call-waiting on your phone.
- Learn the language.
- Let them know who referred you to them.
- Show that you've done research about their company or their services.

- Show that you're listening to them by repeating what they've said to you or echoing their key points.
- Be positive.

Good Opening Lines
- "Here's exactly why I'm calling."
- "Let me get right to the point."
- "Here's the situation."
- "I'm sure you're busy, but I wanted to communicate a quick idea." It's essential that you speak with authority and sound dynamic. Since people also appreciate the entertainment value of all communications, keep in mind that you have to hold their attention by sounding interesting so they're receptive to anything you may have to say. Here in L.A. there is a phrase, "gives good phone," that refers to someone who knows exactly how to use the instrument, and someone whose calls you actually look forward to receiving. They're people who are entertaining, fun, energetic and always have something interesting to say; they respect your time, and they respect their own; they can get the job done.

Don't Do This (Instant Hoopledom!)
- Begin a conversation with a "Hello, who is this?"
- Take more than ten seconds to get to the point.
- Um, hem and haw.
- Have a television on. (This one makes me crazy. At the LASS office we get calls from someone from "XYZ Productions" who is attempting to "big time" us on the phone and I can hear the television and a wailing baby in the background.) Silence, please.
- Say, "Let me get a pencil." Don't pick up the phone unless you're prepared to write!
- Eat or chew gum.
- Use a cheap phone.
- Talk too soft or too loud.
- Lay your lips on the phone.
- Use a speaker phone.
- Lie.
- Mispronounce a name.
- Talk too long.
- Begin your conversation with "Howya doing?" This is a cliché. Do you really care?
- Cop an attitude.

The Basics of Networking by Phone

1. Set aside specific hours to make calls. You really have to be up to do this, so figure out the specific time slot you can be at your verbal optimum to project; for me it's around 11 A.M.

2. Try to make the most of your calls before lunch.

3. It's hard to find music people in their offices on Monday and Friday.

4. Configure an "A" calling list (once a week) of your closest contacts; a "B" list of people to call once a month; and a "C" list for six-month intervals.

5. *Never call someone without something specific to say!*

6. If you're calling to tout your own accomplishments, always begin by focusing on your contact. "I saw an article today which made me think of you," "I was wondering how you were progressing with . . ." Just calling to "touch base" is really not reason enough to call important contacts.

7. Anytime you read something of note about anyone in your network, you have a perfect opportunity to call, as well as an opening: "I saw an article," or "I see you have a song on the new XXX album," or even mention a club listing for a local band. Read everything having to do with your network, especially local music columns, club listings and wedding and birth notices. Look at the list of business announcements (DBAs) in your local paper to see if any music-related businesses have opened their doors.

8. Make all of your calls short, sweet and to the point.

9. Start by indicating that your call is going to be a brief one — "I know you're busy, so I'll keep this short" — is a good way to prepare your listener and allow him to relax, knowing that you're not going to keep him on the phone all day. "I have three things to discuss with you" lets your listener know what to anticipate, also that you're organized and professional.

10. Make notes that you can refer to on your next go-around: "How's that demo going that we discussed?" "How was your gig at the X club?" Don't make it obvious that you're reading from notes; make your contact think that the information he told you a week, a month or even six months ago was important enough for you to remember.

11. Never be afraid to pick up the phone to call someone. Prepare, think what you want to say, and go for it. I know how difficult this can be, but also how necessary. No one can reach out and grab

and shake you over the phone. Be sensitive enough to your listeners to know when they're busy or not into the conversation, but you've got to reach out.

12. If you call someone, it's your responsibility to end the call, always.

13. Never take a call on another line, then return to your original caller and announce how important the call on the other line is. This is very bad form.

14. Listen on the telephone, not just to the words, but to the emotions and sensitivity behind them.

Rolodexes. Invest in a good Rolodex or card file to keep track of your list of contacts and your networking prospects. If you have a computer, design a database form that's easy to use and has enough room to make notes.

Legal pads are good tracking devices too; I use them constantly to transcribe raw information on all my contacts. I keep all of the pads and am surprised how many times they've saved me when I had to refer to information I thought I'd transferred to a more suitable location.

CORRESPONDENCE

It's an old adage that the written word has more credibility than a phone call. The rule of thumb in correspondence is brevity; never write more than one page of anything if you expect a busy person to read it. If you don't have a typewriter or a computer with a word processing program, you should certainly think about making this vital investment as soon as possible. Good-looking stationery, preferably with your own letterhead and matching envelopes, shows the recipient you mean business.

Computers and word processing typewriters are good investments if you plan to generate large quantities of written materials. You can program your basic letter into your word processor and then alter it to meet specific situations, so you won't have to rewrite it each time, and you can keep your submission letters relatively uniform.

On page 90 are some actual sample letters I've written when submitting tapes and press kits to contacts on behalf of my management clients. (I've changed the names and addresses in the interest of privacy.)

Notice in the letter to producer Lou Jeffries on the following page, I

- let the recipient know where we met.
- thanked him for his help.
- reminded him that he requested the information.
- used an exotic close. (The producer works with worldbeat/ exotic acts.) "Mahalo nui" is "thank you" in Hawaiian, and my act is from Honolulu.

Say Thanks Often and Honestly

A thank-you note is the single most effective piece of writing you can send to someone. Believe me, everyone likes to be thanked honestly and sincerely for something they've done. See the following page for an example of a thank-you letter sent to a second engineer who gave above and beyond the call of duty on a recent marathon recording session.

We enclosed this note with a box of chocolate-covered macadamia nuts. Do you think he'll remember us?

The only time to be cautious in sending a thank-you letter is when you're dealing with the press. Here's why.

Journalists have a hard and fast rule about objectivity. If a journalist chooses to cover something it's because he (or his editor) deems it newsworthy. If you send them a thank-you letter you're indicating that they've done you a favor; this violates their code of objectivity.

If a writer has given a favorable review to you or your clients it is permissible to photocopy the article, circle a key phrase, write a note in the margin like "You really nailed it," and send it on. Don't send macadamia nuts.

Postcards

Is there a cheaper way to communicate than the lowly postcard? A postcard can be a wonderful little reminder that you're thinking of someone, and often the funnier or more bizarre it is the better. It's a rare trip home to Lima, Ohio, that I don't pick up a stack of unlikely looking postcards, such lovely pictures as the local oil refinery, a Kmart parking lot, the Lima Mall. I always get amused comments from people I send these slices of Americana to, and they remember them.

May 12, 1993

Bob Leeds
EASTLAKE RECORDING
211 Beverly Blvd.
Hollywood, CA 90093

Dear Bob,

Just a brief note to thank you for your energy and enthusiasm
on last week's session. We certainly couldn't have completed the
tracks or achieved the sound without your help.

I'll look forward to working with you soon; please feel free to
use me as a reference for any prospective clients.

Sincerely,

Dan Kim

May 20, 1993

Lou Jeffries
923 S. Clark Dr.
Beverly Hills, CA 90211

Dear Lou,

I enjoyed meeting you at the Wailing Souls video shoot at
Descano Gardens on Friday. Thanks for your insight—the
information will be helpful in putting together the Music
Connection article.

Find enclosed the tape on my management client that you
requested. I've also enclosed some press and bio information.

Thanks for your interest, Lou.

Mahalo nui,

Dan Kimpel
DKM Management

A friend in PR suggests having a stack of stamped postcards on your desk to send out to networking acquaintances; don't think about it, just do it.

On Cold Contact Letters

I've seen songwriters and artists prepare fairly elaborate response cards to inquire about music business submissions. Response cards are preprinted postcards that are enclosed with inquiry letters to music publishers and record companies to find out about their material submission policies. They ask:

- If the company is accepting material
- How many songs to send
- What type of material is needed
- What format to send (although cassette is standard)
- If material will be returned with an SASE (self-addressed, stamped envelope)

Although a response card may help some songwriters or artists find out about the possibility of sending unsolicited material, it's been my experience that a telephone call is generally more expedient. Always contact the company to get the name, including its pronunciation and spelling, and exact title of the person who listens to incoming submissions. "Attention A&R" or "Professional Manager" is the greeting of an amateur, so know the person's name.

Since I believe in networking as the most viable way into the music business, I can't believe that blindly sending out tapes to record companies is the best way to advance your career. You need personal contacts. The best way to begin your search for these in the maze of record and publishing companies (many of whom will listen to unsolicited material) is with the venerable *Songwriter's Market* published by Writer's Digest Books.

Always send follow-up letters to contacts as soon as possible. Don't delay, especially if you've just met someone who wants to hear your tape or other materials. As you probably know, most people have remarkably short attention spans and memories, so send a letter the week you've met someone, and follow up the letter with a call as soon as you're sure they've had time to listen to your material, probably within another week. When you call, remind them again of what you've sent, because if they can't immediately recall your submission, you may be helping them out of a potentially embarrassing situation. Your window of contact only stays open for a certain period of time. Waiting six months to call someone you met briefly on one occasion may make them question your business sense. Contacting them within a shorter period of time is more normal.

The Name Game

Everyone likes to have his or her name pronounced and spelled correctly as well as remembered. When you meet people in a networking situation, it's important to instantly commit their name to memory. Repetition is the key here; say their name at least three times in the conversation. Keep a small notepad in your possession and make notes, surreptitiously if you can. That way you know exactly who you've encountered and when. Never be afraid to ask someone for a business card, but be aware of subtle and not so subtle signs. I've seen A&R people and publishers claim that they're "fresh out." This usually means a temporarily closed door for the aspirant. I once watched a record company executive walk through a music industry convention with his name-bearing badge turned around, so no one would know who he was and attempt to engage him in dialogue or give him tapes.

When you write to someone, it's important to know their title; don't trust your resource materials 100 percent. If you're submitting to a record company, a publisher or the media, call and ask the receptionist the exact title. Titles are subject to change, and sending something to Bill Jones, "A&R Manager" if it should be Bill Jones "Vice President of A&R" will create a negative impression. You want the recipients of your efforts to know that you're aware of their position in the company.

Business Cards

A great-looking business card is a pretty good investment. The availability of computers and laser printers make designing your own card fairly easy, and print shops also have facilities and professional expertise. Make sure your card is readable; avoid bizarre or limiting type styles and keep it very, very simple. When you move or change phone numbers, get new cards. Please don't cross out the old phone number and continue to use the card; it's tacky and amateurish. Avoid clichés in your description of what you do, and don't attempt to consolidate too many of your various identities on one card. If you wear more than one hat, get more than one business card; it won't break the bank.

You will also want to avoid tacky clip art that hasn't changed since the 1950s. Tired-looking music notes and spinning records fall into this category. Look at the type styles and designs in current magazines. Cut out the type styles and graphics you think would be suitable for you, and use these as examples to emulate or show to your typesetter.

Keep your business cards in a holder designed for this purpose; they won't get dog-eared and they'll be easily accessible.

COMMUNICATING WITH THE PRESS

The press is a valuable ally. Learn the art of communicating with them via well-written press releases. On the following page are two examples of materials written for the same event.

The Calendar Listing

Calendar listings give just the who, what, where, when and why. In the market I work, this has to be received at least three weeks in advance of the event. This information is to be sent directly to the individual who is responsible for compiling, editing and placing it in the publication. Find out the name and title of this person by calling the publication.

The Press Release

A press release is written in a more literary and descriptive style. It also incorporates the who, what, when, where and why, but in addition it should give the harassed editor a handle on writing something about the event with a minimum of thought. It's been my experience that often the press release becomes the article, so make the release as complete as possible. Direct your releases to the appropriate contact; don't send the news editor an entertainment release for example. It is entirely permissable to call to make sure that the information was received. If your contact claims they didn't receive it, be prepared to resend or fax the information again.

The way to interest the press is to create newsworthy events for them to cover. "Band plays club, ten people come and drink" is not worthy of press attention. You've got to think about their needs, not just yours.

Memorize the differences between the following:

KEO BRINGS THE ISLANDS TO THE MAINLAND

The Lotus Festival, presented by the City of Los Angeles to
celebrate the contributions of Asian/Pacific Islanders to the
metropolitan cultural landscape, is proud to announce the
signing of Hawaiian Worldpop artist Keo as their headline
attraction. Keo will appear on Saturday, July 11, at 5:00 PM on
the main stage at Echo Park. In recent years this festival has
attracted over 100,000 participants throughout the weekend,
according to the festival's entertainment chairperson Patrick
Strong.

Keo's show combines hard-hitting contemporary pop music with
African, Brazilian and Hawaiian overtones. He incorporates
dancers in a ferocious display of ethnic dance and street funk
while his potent seven-piece band lays down a fiery tribal
backbeat.

Keo's m
intentior
audience
concerne
his your
him an
free and
used to
smaller

CALENDAR OR LISTING EDITOR
JUNE 15 FOR IMMEDIATE RELEASE
CONTACT: Dan Kimpel, (213) 555-0599

WHO: Keo
WHAT: Hawaiian Worldpop singer
WHERE: The Lotus Festival at Echo Park (11 Glendale Blvd.,
North end of the lake between Glendale & Park Blvd.)
WHEN: Saturday, July 11, at 5:00 PM
WHY: The Lotus Festival, in its 15th year, is a two-day event
sponsored by the City of Los Angeles Parks and Recreation
Department and Sprint to celebrate the contributions of
Asian/Pacific Islanders to the Los Angeles cultural landscape
with music, dance, art, crafts and food.

BACKGROUND:
Keo's music is hard-hitting contemporary pop with African,
Latin and Hawaiian overtones. He incorporates dancers in a
ferocious display of ethnic dance and street funk while his
seven-piece band lays down a fiery tribal backbeat. The Lotus
Festival affords audiences a rare opportunity to hear Keo in a
free concert which celebrates musical multiculturalism and the
unifying power of global rhythm.

Advertising: the purchase of space in a paper or magazine to let readers know about an event, product or service.

Publicity: hard news coverage occuring before the event. Is there a newsworthy aspect (Is it the first event of its kind? The only?) that will help get coverage?

Promotion: putting up flyers, posters; sending direct mail.

Public relations: a response to your event in the form of a story through the eyes, pen or camera of an electronic or print journalist.

In order to pitch the media on your event, band or service you've got to write a short pitch letter, send a complete and professional press kit, and make sure that you're targeting the proper outlet for the information.

The Mini-Feature

The addition of a mini-feature, or canned story, can certainly make your pitch much stronger. On the following page is a mini-feature that I wrote for a client. He uses this material as part of his press kit. I also developed an edited "one-sheet," using key paragraphs, which is sent out to program directors of radio stations and magazines with his record.

This mini-feature works because Harold Payne's music is actually as interesting as I described it. He'd had other press kit items written for him which he didn't like because they were too exclusive. Notice that as flattering as the descriptions are I didn't use superlatives: They have no place in press materials.

If you don't have a record out, don't bother trying to place stories in the national media. It does absolutely no good to have a story in a high-profile medium if there's not an item for the reader to purchase; it's a waste of time and energy. Save major press for when you have a record to promote.

Only use the local media when you have an event that readers can go to, or a product they can purchase easily, preferably as soon as they read about it! Keep in mind that in our media-inundated society, the more sources you can use to imprint your information on the general public the better. It often takes at least three separate sources of information to make a lasting impact on someone; even then they may not know where they got the information.

If you're going to pitch the media on your projects, make sure you've got the right person on the line. The entertainment editor is your surest bet and is someone who actually has an office at the

HAROLD PAYNE PASSES IT ON

One hundred years ago, Harold Payne would have jumped freight
trains or stowed away on tramp steamers. He could have written
novels like Jack London, painted portraits of exotic native
womanhood like Paul Gauguin, and been a guide through steaming
jungles from the farthest outposts of known civilization.

In these days of the jet plane, Harold Payne uses songs, his
voice and a guitar to traverse a global road that has led him from
Chiang Mai to Moscow, from Bali to Bora-Bora. He's worked on film
scores in India, toured Japan, and appeared as a regular on
Australian television. He's sung in Singapore, he's strummed in
Samoa, he's dreamt in Hindu temples, and jammed with the itinerant
street musicians of Ireland: he shares it with us on his new Affinity
Records release Pass It On.

Harold Payne's global orientation came to him naturally as he
grew up in the multicultural melting pot of Gardena, California.
Growing up with Japanese, Hawaiian, Afro-American and Mexican
neighbors allowed Harold an intimate glimpse into other cultures, and
to experience a broad geographical spectrum of music.

On the homefront, Payne's songs have garnered over 100
cover versions for other artists. His song "I Wish He Didn't Trust Me
So Much" reached the #2 spot on the Billboard R&B charts for Bobby
Womack, and singers from Patti LaBelle to the Cover Girls have
brought Harold's songs to the public via radio and record mediums.
Motion pictures Beverly Hills Cop II, Splash and Summer Rental are
just a few of the films with which Harold has been involved
musically. His group "Gravity" has toured to support their successful
album release in Japan, and Harold co-wrote "Music Speaks Louder
Than Words" the theme song for the Songwriter Summit held in the
former Soviet Union, where Payne and top songwriters including
Cindi Lauper, Brenda Russell, Michael Bolton and Barry Mann met in

album Pass It On. A rich and sophisticated musical patina paints the
sound with acoustic guitars, choral vocal harmonies and sparkling
synthesizers providing the frame for Payne's husky heartfelt vocals.
The songs on this collection, recorded with different producers in
various studios in Los Angeles, are unified through the songwriting.
In the world of Harold Payne the songs are the most important
element ("the song is king" he states simply) and the ten selections
on Pass It On are so genuine and natural they sound as if they may
have written themselves. The chance encounter, the moment that
might have been, the distances between lovers, physical and
emotional, and the solitary view where the city lights recede from the
window of an airplane and blend into the stars over a dark ocean are
all here.

So Harold Payne continues: to write, to celebrate, to travel, to
perform and to make a musical difference. The positivity of his music
is bound to affect audiences, whether they're longtime fans or brand-
new listeners. "We can make a difference...a single candle in the
night can turn the darkness into light," he sings, and by allowing us
to share his musical vision he lets us commune with that warmth,
and to experience the power of his singular musical vision.

publication; many times freelancers or contributing editors work out of their homes and for more than one publication. Receptionists will freely give you the appropriate editor's name if you use the telephone techniques described in this chapter to sound authoritative. If you invite the media to an event, give them ample time, make the event sound as interesting as possible, and follow-up the week before the event. You can check to see if the materials you sent arrived and verbally reinforce your pitch. The offices of many major magazines resemble Auntie Em's farm after the tornado, so materials are easily misplaced or misfiled. Know the type of person you're dealing with, and be prepared to do the thinking for them; they may not know where your project falls in terms of how to cover it. Tell them. Have confidence and enthusiasm, and keep in mind that timing is of the essence.

Stories can fall into place in ways you might not imagine. I recently pitched a client to a magazine which agreed, rather disinterestedly, that they'd do "something." Two days before their scheduled deadline their cover story/interview fell through, so the small story they'd anticipated writing about my client was now on the cover. They had to scramble to interview him by phone, but we had much more space in the magazine than we'd ever expected.

If You Want Something Done Right . . .

In promoting upcoming shows, events and gigs never rely on anyone, even a reputable public relations firm, to do your work for you. I had this illustrated to me just this morning when I received a fax from a PR firm concerning a multi-artist outdoor concert with one of my acts on the bill. The PR agency sent me a fax of a memo they'd received from the promoter of the show instructing them to provide bios and pictures to the press; my act wasn't one of those designated to receive this special attention.

However, I'd already serviced the press with the show information, featuring my act's bio, picture and a media-ready press release. Every music magazine in southern California already had this information, sent well in advance of the show since I knew each publication's lead time, with my act listed first. I had also made friends within the PR agency and let them understand that I was there to work with them in the promotion of my act as well as the overall event. (I doubt if any of the other acts' management companies had ingratiated themselves in this way.) Consequently, my act received the greatest amount of advance press for the event and appeared to be the headliner, even if the promoter didn't necessarily see it that way.

I was able to add the PR firm to my network, as well as to use my pre-existent press network to give me coverage for my act; we were able to make the show's press a major coup.

I have a friend on the road as the tour coordinator with a mid-level urban act. They were performing in Philadelphia, and she'd sent a fax to the promoter which clearly showed the time that their entourage would be arriving at the airport, the size of their party, how large a limo they'd need, and how big a passenger and equipment van for the musicians and crew. After sending the fax, she followed up by calling the promoter to make sure he'd received it; he assured her he had. The next day when the twenty-person entourage arrived at the airport, there was no one there to meet them; the star was livid. When the tour manager called the promoter, he admitted that even though he'd received the fax he'd neglected to read it and thought they were arriving the next day! That's rock and roll. My friend maintained her job, barely, but she learned a valuable lesson.

Musicians will be late, trucks will be towed away, flyers won't be ready on time, names will be misspelled, mics will fall on the floor, and the promoter will owe you money; such is the way of the music world. Rather than letting this depress you, even momentarily, anticipate disasters, but don't overanticipate. Have enough confidence in your own abilities to work and make correct instinctive decisions under pressure so that you'll be ready for whatever may occur in the line of fire, because that's the reality of this business.

This Really Happened Department. Two months ago I sent a press kit and tape on a client to a specialized local magazine in Los Angeles. When I called the next week, I asked for the editor to whom I'd sent the materials. The receptionist was very guarded and said he wasn't there; when I asked when he'd be in, she said "Do you know him?" When I admitted I didn't, she let loose with this information: "He died last week. Is there anyone else who can help you?" My first impulse was to try to make light of this, but my inner critic thankfully prevailed and I could only whisper, "I'm so sorry." I was referred to another editor (his successor) and actually ended up getting a cover story for my client. Be prepared for these situations, not just deaths, but firings, promotions, transfers, etc.

You Can Lead a Journalist to Water . . .

When I began doing public relations for actual clients, I learned one lesson fast. One of my first clients was an author/educator who had just published a book. I contacted the media, sent out press releases and press copies, and got reviews in a number of magazines. The only problem is that not all of the magazines felt positively about the book. One of the reviews in fact was downright evil.

Fortunately, my client and I, throughout two separate lifetimes in the entertainment industry, have developed the emotions of zombies when it comes to the criticism of our work. I would suggest that you do the same if you're going to be involved in public relations and promotion of events. Critics are paid to offer their opinions, and not everyone is going to like what they see. Our goals as creative people should never be to please all of the people all of the time, because that means that we're rounding off all of the edges on our work simply to appease popular tastes. In the culinary world when you do this you've created a bland, processed hamburger. In the music business you're creating bland, processed elevator music.

Don't worry too much about bad press. Negative reviews have a way of leaving the mind of the reader, and essentially what they remember is the name of the product, not necessarily one writer's negative opinion of it.

Wrap Up

Sales, persuasion, public relations and hype are not dirty words. They are necessary ingredients in the positive development of your career, and in your life. It is essential that you have enough self-awareness to realize which of your traits are most salable. You may have to step outside yourself to see that if you're banging your head against a rock maybe it's time to walk around it, to pursue things in a new adventurous way and to chart your own course.

Belief is the strongest selling point of all, so only commit yourself to what you truly believe in, and use every power you can conjure up to convince others that you're right. Use your imagination, and trust your instincts and perceptions.

CHAPTER SIX

PUTTING IT ALL TOGETHER

At this point in the book you've probably come up with some ideas for applying the information I've given you to your own career. As I've mentioned, there is no standard set of rules for doing things in the music industry—only guidelines can be provided—it's up to you to make them work for you.

The following is a personal checklist: Assess yourself as honestly as you can when considering these questions.

FOR PERFORMERS AND SONGWRITERS

1. **Is your career the most important thing in your life?** As we've discussed throughout this book, the individuals who are successful as performers in the music business all share a single-minded resolve and commitment to their music. Is your resolve exemplified through your single-minded devotion to your career?

2. **Are you unique enough to succeed?** In the music business, performers are defined by what they create; it's essential that the image presented to a potential audience is a unique one. Yes, the music business is always looking for "the next big thing," but they may not know it when they see it. It's up to you to define your image through music, video, performance, fashion and a unique statement.

3. **Is your music honestly better than what is currently available on record?** Your music has to be unique. Re-creating something that currently exists may provide you with a living in clubs, but it won't help you to convince a record company that there is an untapped market for your music. You have to bring the music from your imagination and heart to connect with people who will accept, understand and market it.

4. **Can you explain who your audience is? (Performers)** Even though you're unique, you should be able to identify a radio

format that will play your music and expose you to an audience of buyers. The baby boomers whose buying power made the record business what it is don't currently buy much new rock product, so billions of dollars of CD technology have been utilized to rerecord the hits of the 1960s and 1970s to sell to this audience. The current boom in country music can be attributed to older buyers who are alienated from hard rock and rap music; country with a rock edge is a logical choice for these listeners. New age music is providing an outlet for creative artists who previously wouldn't have fit into a pre-existing format. College radio has been instrumental in breaking more radical bands for teenagers, still the largest buyers of prerecorded music.

5. Is your audience a record-buying one? (Performers) This relates to our previous point; record companies are in the business of selling records, period. Fortunately for artists who may not fit into traditional formats, there is alternative marketing; mail order and point-of-purchase concert sales can help an act generate revenue and credibility while climbing the ladder to success. These avenues will be significant in proving to a label that there is a market for your music.

6. Are you young enough to have a long career in the music industry? (Performers) Many of the acts being signed today are in their teens and early twenties, as has always been the case with popular music. A young audience identifies with young performers. Even though there are older bands who tour and record successfully, their audience has grown up with them. In the history of show business, many performers have altered their ages downward, to give themselves an edge in appealing to a younger market. One reason that record companies may be reluctant to sign an older artist is the perception that he has already fulfilled his growth cycle, so the input that he receives from producers, A&R, etc., won't have much impact on his music; he has finished developing. Bands and performers who are younger will always have an advantage in getting signed, but there have always been, and will always be, exceptions to this rule. It's gratifying when talent and hard work win out to expose a new, though not so young, artist. Witness the success of journeyman singer/songwriter Michael Bolton.

7. Does the individuality of your looks qualify you for video stardom? (Performers) Videos have put the faces of artists in front of millions of people. Because rock and roll has always been more about individuality of looks rather than glamour, performers have to invent styles that fit with their music. A performer should learn about movement and motion in order to present his best visual image to the cameras.

8. **Are you investing enough of your income into your career?** You are responsible for investing in your success. You'll need demos; if you're a performer, you'll also need pictures, press kits, videos and costumes. You may need to pay musicians or publicists; you need to be resourceful in making your money stretch as far as possible. As we discussed in the previous chapter, bartering can help you achieve your goals, but seed money is necessary to start any business.

9. **Do others share your enthusiasm?** We, as creative people, can't operate in a vacuum. We require inspiration from those around us. If you're not getting this from your current network, you need either to expand it or devote your energies to making music that reaches more people, particularly those who can add their energies to your project.

10. **Can you generate loyalty in others?** You need support from a network; you will need to inspire others to stay with you through your growth period, and through the potentially lean economic times. Let those who you trust and respect influence you with their artistic input into your project. The best possible way to convince others to be loyal to you is by being loyal to them and encouraging their efforts too.

11. **Can you make audiences crazy? (Performers)** Rock and roll is a kinetic experience where performers and audience merge. Country music performers are often singers who the audience can imagine sitting down and drinking a beer with after the show. Other forms of music may explore the relationship between audience and performer a little differently, but audiences certainly have to respond to what you do in order for you to be successful.

Most record companies need to see performers live before signing them. Therefore the chemistry that you create onstage is vital to your success as an artist, particularly in rock and roll and country music. You have to pay some dues, to work in front of audiences as often as possible to learn what you do best to connect with them. Do whatever is necessary to make them respond to you. Use your imagination; this is show business.

12. **Are you experiencing artistic growth?** Creative people

need to change and evolve. Open up to new influences, musically, visually, conceptually. Try new things, talk to different people, work with different co-writers and musicians; don't get in a rut.

13. **Are you actively involved in the study of dance, voice or songwriting at this time?** Expanding and honing your abilities is rewarding, not only in your career, but in your life. If you're in a location where you don't have access to classes or workshops, can you create informal ones with your networking contacts? Informal songwriting workshops can be very stimulating; they will also give you one of the key motivational reasons to create: you'll have an outlet.

14. **Do you read books that can educate you about your career?** We are fortunate to live in an era when information about the music business is so readily accessible. Make a list of books to read; buy them, borrow them, or convince your local library to order them for you and any other aspiring reader who will learn from reading them.

15. **Do you work at achieving maximum outreach by calling managers, publishers, agents, etc.?** Sometimes it's difficult to motivate ourselves to make the calls and meet the people we need to meet. If you're using a goal list, as discussed in chapter four, designate a specific time for outreach; write down the calls to be made each week and religiously apply yourself to completing this list.

16. **Does everyone on the local level know who you are?** You've got to lay your groundwork locally before you can be successful nationally and globally. Don't let the light of future success blind you to helpful folks around you; they can lead you to their contacts, and help you expand your network. Don't be jealous of successful performers in your hometown; network with them and use their success to expand your own network.

17. **Do you need to relocate to another city to be successful?** If you need to do it, do it. Plan, research and visit first though; the more contacts you have the better. Be realistic with your time goals in your chosen city; you won't experience overnight success. Also, take advantage of the fact that you can now reinvent yourself.

18. **Are you afraid of succeeding?** Fear of success shows itself in many ways, but mostly through not doing what you know you need to do. Trust your instincts. One prominent Grand Dame dance mistress, when asked by young dancers if they should pursue a

full-time career in dance, would invariably answer "no." She had determined that if they had to ask her, then they hadn't made up their own minds; therefore, they didn't have the necessary ambition or confidence in their abilities to succeed.

19. Are you consciously or unconsciously sabotaging your career? You can sabotage yourself in obvious or subtle ways with the same result. By not doing what you know you need to do, by working with negative and unsupportive people, using drugs and alcohol, allowing yourself to be separated from your music, prostituting your talents and getting in a rut, you telegraph to others that you don't want to be successful.

FOR SUPPORT PERSONNEL

1. Are you doing everything possible to educate yourself about this business? Volunteering or interning, reading, studying *Billboard* magazine, and taking classes are just a few of the ways to learn more about the business. Also, going out and hearing music as often as possible, meeting the people who create it locally, and finding your niche should be your priorities.

2. Do you have the financial resources to direct into your career? Just as the potential hit recording artist needs to invest in himself, so do you. The more you have to offer the members of your network, the more valuable you'll be. Having a good piece of equipment, a video camera, a photo studio or a computer will give you bartering leverage.

3. Can you hear the hits? If you're going to manage bands or work in an administrative support capacity, you've got to have a clear instinct about what makes a band or performer viable in the marketplace. Try listening to new records and predicting which ones will be Top 10 hits. Listen carefully to establish the patterns shared by the top records: writing, production, musicianship, subject matter.

4. Do you have vision? Are you able to envision your success and share that vision with others? Successful managers can work with their acts to develop long-term plans. It's impossible to see into the future, but creating goals can help to shape it.

5. Are you an active or a reactive person? Active people take action, have plans and are aggressive. Reactive people respond to the opportunities placed before them. Most successful music business entrepreneurs are active people.

6. Can you direct others to do what you need? You need to be forceful enough to command others, and charismatic enough that they'll want to do what you want. If they like you, respect you, and trust your judgment, this will be relatively simple.

7. Are you a good salesperson? As discussed in chapter five, sales can determine your success. Devote your attention to this function; your ability to sell can give you an in to the business. In a creative scene, there is often a glut of creative talent and a shortage of people who know how to present and sell it.

8. Do you present yourself effectively? Clothes, physical bearing and social skills all telegraph who we are to others before we say a word. Look and act the part of a music industry professional. Observe those around you who are successful in this business. What traits do they share that you have or can develop?

9. Are your verbal skills representative of your intellect? The words that we use in conversation are one of the primary ways that we're judged. Listen to yourself in conversation; do you use too much slang or profanity? You can expand your vocabulary by using a thesaurus or dictionary, by writing down interesting and descriptive words you see in magazines and newspapers, and then adding them to your vocabulary.

10. Are your writing skills up to par? A typing class in high school or college can be invaluable in later life, and computer skills are a prerequisite in the current marketplace. But knowing *what* to write is certainly as important as knowing how. Familiarize yourself with standard business letters; practice writing press releases and bios as shown in chapter five of this book, either for yourself, your acts or potential clients.

11. Are you aggressive? You need chutzpah to be successful in any business. Being aggressive doesn't mean being confrontational or abrasive, but you have to ask for what you want and be relentless in coming up with ways to get it.

12. Are you aligning yourself with the right people? You will interact with an expansive network of individuals who possess a variety of talents, personalities and aspirations. Your contacts are a reflection of you; you have to be able to advance your career by interacting with them. Make sure that you are around people who' are as positive and creative as you wish to be.

13. Are you positive? You will certainly get back what you give out; so you need to generate positivity in those that you encounter. If you find that your outlook is negative, ascertain why it is and determine what you need to do to change it.

14. Can you create plans and keep to them until they're completed? Before you chart a course, you first need to plan it; otherwise, you're just being blown to where the strongest winds may take you. In a career in the music business you can't anticipate everything that's going to influence you, but you can plan weekly, monthly and yearly goals.

15. Do you listen to and chart trends in music? Can you name the top-selling artists of this year? What trends are currently bubbling under the surface that are most likely to become major sources of revenue for record labels this year? Music works on cycles, and what is happening on the top of the charts influences everything else beneath it.

16. Do you read at least three music industry magazines a week? Go to your local library, subscribe to magazines or stand at the newsstand and read until the proprieter asks you to leave; there is new information every week; you need to know it.

17. Do you have access to a music industry resource library, and use it? Some local songwriting organizations pool their resources to purchase books and periodicals which the members share. Do you know others who would be interested in sharing materials with you in such a relationship?

18. Can you work locally? Strong grass roots are vital to national movements. Meet your local movers and shakers and begin to network with them; let them know what you do and create situations to work together. Create a scene.

19. Are you in the right place geographically? You have to go where it is. If you need to live in a major music capitol, don't arrive broke, and do your homework. Don't go to New York to work with country artists, or to Nashville to do rap.

If you've answered negatively to more than four questions, you may need to re-evaluate your commitment to success. Your ambition, energy and resourcefulness are the tools which will determine your potential. You can certainly change and improve to succeed; establish your goals, fuel your motivation and figure an angle to position yourself for success.

I know we've all met people in our lives who tell us they look back with regret that they didn't attempt something they could have accomplished. They will live out the rest of their lives with the feeling that maybe, if they'd just tried, they could have been successful at something very special. If you are determined to succeed in the music business, you will find a way.

MUSIC INDUSTRY TRADE EVENTS

The following is a list of noteworthy events where rabid industry networking is the key activity. You should contact the organizations listed for information about their events. You can also check to see if it's possible to trade volunteer time in exchange for admission to events, since qualified, enthusiastic people are usually required to staff them.

Some organizations, such as the Los Angeles Songwriters Show-case Songwriters Expo, will provide limited free admissions to organizations and publications who can assist in promoting their event via print ads in local papers or organization newsletters.

If you belong to a local organization that publishes a newsletter, you can also try to obtain a press pass to cover an event. Tip: Many organizers prefer that you provide publicity before their events, not after.

AES Convention
(212) 661-8528
Audio Engineering Society
60 E. 42nd St.
New York, NY 10117
A biannual convention for engineers and audio manufacturers, this even attracts technical personnel who have an opportunity to see, hear and experience the newest in studio technology.

CMJ Music Marathon
(516) 466-6000
245 Great Neck Rd., 3rd Floor
Long Island City, NY 11021
Fall convention for college and alternative radio with seminars, exhibitions, live showcases and the CMJ Music Awards. College

radio has been instrumental in the past five years in helping the careers of bands too strange for mainstream radio. If you have an indie release and are seeking airplay for new, innovative product, this is a good bet for you. The major performing rights organizations all attend, as do record label A&R.

DJ Expo
(516) 767-2500
Testa Communications
25 Willowdale Ave.
Port Washington, NY 11050
A convention for club/radio DJs and club owners. Dance music affords some of the most valuable opportunities for producers and artists working with independent records. Many trends that become mainstream first appear in the clubs. With the rise of technology, there is a whole new species called "remixers" who take commercial releases, then alter and beef them up for the dance floor. Dance music is one of the most experimental popular music forms.

Foundations Forum
(212) 645-1360
1133 Broadway, Suite 204
New York, NY 10010
This fall event is held in Los Angeles for musicians, managers and producers working in the rock and heavy metal formats. There are panels and workshops covering everything from censorship to legal advice. This event has been growing by leaps and bounds in the last couple of years, and is highly regarded by those in the black leather and tattoo contingent.

Gavin Convention
(415) 495-1990
Gavin Report
140 2nd St.
San Francisco, CA 94105
Radio/record promotion conference.

MIDEM
(212) 750-8899
International Exhibition Organization, Inc.
475 Park Ave. S., 30th Floor
New York, NY 10016

International record distribution and music publishing trade event held in January in Cannes, France. MIDEM is the largest international convention for the record industry. It's a madhouse of buyers, sellers and middlemen all speaking in a dozen languages. If you have product you wish to expose to the European market, this is an opportunity to meet the international record business.

MusicFest
Presented by the Rocky Mountain Music Association
231 Harrison St.
Denver, CO 80206
Songwriters conference and trade event in June sponsored by ASCAP.

NAIRD Convention
(609) 547-3331
National Association of Independent Record Distributors & Manufacturers
P.O. Box 568
Maple Shade, NJ 08052
Convention in May for independent distributor/label personnel.

NAMM
National Association of Music Merchants
(800) 767-NAMM
Winter NAMM convention in January in Anaheim, California. A gigantic convention of the latest music gear, it attracts equipment merchandisers and retailers from across the country. There are always plenty of celebrities on hand too, generally endorsing their gear of choice. This event really must be seen to be believed. It occupies literally acres of space and creates a cacophony that will leave an indelible print on your eardrums. This event is not open to the general public, but the press and representatives of retail/wholesale audio and musical products are welcome. There are many creative ways to attend this event, and it's well worth it to see the state of the instrument business.

NARM Conference
National Association of Recording Merchandisers
(609) 596-2221
11 Eves Dr., Suite 140
Marlton, NJ 08053

New Music America/Montreal
Musiques Actuelles
(514) 499-1990
3575 Boul. Saint-Laurent, Suite 240
Montreal, Quebec, H2X 217 Canada
November event.

New Music Seminar
(212) 473-4343
632 Broadway, 9th Floor
New York, NY 10012
International music extravaganza for indie artists, managers, producers, etc., with seminars, lectures and panels. New Music Nights
are held in showcase clubs throughout New York during the convention and feature a zillion bands crammed into every club in New
York City. You'll meet all strata of business at this event, and since
your seminar pass gives you access to all of the clubs, you can stay
out late (clubs in NYC close at 4 A.M.; then you go afterhours) and
hear the latest bands from a variety of major and independent record
labels.

Northern California Songwriters Association Conference
(415) 327-8296
855 Oak Grove Ave., Suite 211
Menlo Park, CA 94025
October event hosted by BMI, ASCAP, SESAC. It has been growing;
publishers and record people come up from Los Angeles, and although the northern California music scene isn't as influential as
L.A.'s, there is a lot of music happening. This event is for songwriters, so expect to hear songs galore.

SMPTE Annual Conference
(914) 761-1100
Society of Motion Picture & Television Engineers
595 W. Hartsdale Ave
White Plains, NY 10607
A high-end, technical convention, this event attracts engineers and
studio owners from across the country.

Songwriters Expo
(213) 467-7823

LASS
P.O. Box 93759
Hollywood, CA 90093
Fall event. It's the largest educational discovery event for writers and music industry professionals held in North America. The Expo is two intensive days of classes, panels and workshops with many of the most acclaimed and recorded songwriters in North America. There is a booth area where representatives of songwriting organizations and companies who market items for writers meet with the participants one-on-one. Expos have been held since 1976, making it one of the longest-running shows in the music biz. The only negative thing about this event is that there is almost too much going on; you'll need to sleep for a week afterwards.

South By Southwest
(512) 467-7979
P.O. Box 4999
Austin, Texas 78765
Music business trade/seminars for independent musicians held in early spring. Austin is a music center with a phenomenal live performing scene. Certain bands and artists have emerged from Austin, but it's viewed as a purer music center than New York, Los Angeles or Nashville. Most of the club activities, which are in full swing during South By Southwest, take place on Sixth Street, which is wall to wall live music venues. The music tends to be pretty original, though roots rock, blues and folk are all well represented.

West L.A. Music Keyboard Expo
(310) 477-1945
11345 Santa Monica Blvd.
Los Angeles, CA 90025
Keyboard and equipment fall expo. This event bills itself as a "musicians NAMM" which indicates that it is a two-day event featuring all of the latest gear, MIDI and recording equipment, and instruments for musicians. A healthy smattering of celebrity rocks show up, and this event has grown steadily since its inception.

MUSIC INDUSTRY PUBLICATIONS

We read magazines not only for entertainment, but because they provide a lifeline to the music industry. I recommend the following to help educate you about the business:

American Songwriter
42 Music Square West
Nashville, TN 37203
A rare magazine indeed, one geared to songwriters. Based in Nashville, *American Songwriter* covers the national music scene admirably in bimonthly issues. Journalism is concise and relevant, and there have been some interesting special issues. The interviews are usually excellent, and a number of columns cover the activities not only in Music City but across the country.

BAM Magazine
5951 Canning St.
Oakland, CA 94609
Based in northern California, the magazine also has a southern California edition. The publication is by subscription, but free at drop sites locally. They also produce the BAMMIES, the Bay-area music awards. *BAM*'s emphasis is on hard-hitting metal and rock and roll with a substantial number of pages given to full-page ads purchased by bands or promoters. The publication previews upcoming shows and has record and concert reviews.

The Beat
% Bongo Productions
P.O. Box 65856
Los Angeles, CA 90065
For anyone interested in the exploding global music scene, this visionary publication is a must-read. Covering African, Brazilian, Indian and Reggae music plus every other applicable world music form, this magazine is fascinating for musicians wanting to touch the deeper wellspring. Originally devoted to reggae, recent editions have covered everything from East Indians to Tahitian choral music. The graphics are well done, the writing very personal, and there are records reviewed here that will never end up in your local Kmart.

Billboard
1515 Broadway, 39th Floor
New York, NY 10036
The essential weekly trade journal. Buy, beg or borrow it, or better yet, convince your local library to carry this magazine — this is required reading. Current editor Timothy White maintains the in-

tegrity of this venerable publication with on-the-money editorials. Learn to read the charts where every type of music, from the top 200 to hits from Europe and Asia, are represented. All signings and assignments of music industry personnel are listed, as well as births and deaths. It reports signings and trends and includes feature stories. This is the storehouse of information you need to access to be in the music business.

Billboard International Talent and Touring Directory
Billboard Publications
1 Astor Plaza
1515 Broadway
New York, NY 10036
Published annually, listing artists, booking agents, etc.

Cashbox
157 W. 57th St., Suite 1402
New York, NY 10019
A companion to *Billboard*, *Cashbox* is a venerable magazine, and a very informative weekly journal about the music business. Record reviews, radio notes and inside information are included.

Creem
4735 Sepulveda Blvd., Suite 49
Sherman Oaks, CA 91403
Now in a new incarnation, this magazine began as an alternative Detroit-based magazine back in the late 1960s, got teenie, and now is back in a new format as a semi-alternative publication.

Daily Variety
1400 N. Cahuenga Blvd.
Hollywood, CA 90028
More movie/TV oriented, there's enough cross-collaterialization with the music world to make it important reading.

Dance Music Report
3339 22nd St.
Long Island City, NY 11106

Downbeat
180 W. Park Ave. S., Suite 105
Elmhurst, Il 60126
The long-standing publication for jazz players; very hip.

Entertainment Law Reporter
2210 Wilshire Blvd., #311
Santa Monica, CA 90403

Guitar Player
20085 Stevens Creek Blvd.
Cupertino, CA 95014
Guitar as big business — a wonderful publication for the six-stringer.

Guitar World
1115 Broadway, 8th Floor
New York, NY 10010

Hits
(818) 501-7900
15477 Ventura Blvd., Suite 300
Sherman Oaks, CA 91403
An expensive, very inside weekly magazine with a wonderful sense of humor that results in some very entertaining reading. Classic photo captions. Highly recommended for readers who want to see how the record industry views and reports on itself with tongue firmly in cheek. You can learn who the players are here.

Hollywood Reporter
6715 Sunset Blvd.
Hollywood, CA 90028
A daily magazine, they publish special editions throughout the year. Their music for television and movies edition, containing information for music people, is a must-have.

Home & Studio Recording
7318 Topanga Canyon Blvd., Suite 200
Canoga Park, CA 91303
Super nice people run this "user friendly" publication; very informative reading for the musician/producer. A section called "Our Readers' Tapes" gives demo critiques. This magazine has expanded to include columns on songwriting as well as production.

International Musician
1501 Broadway, Suite 600
New York, NY 10036

Keyboard
20085 Stevens Creek Blvd.
Cupertino, CA 95014
Talk about equipment lust; this magazine provides it full out. A
must-have for the serious keyboard player. Interesting product reviews and transcriptions of charts.

Mix Magazine
6400 Hollis St., #12
Emeryville, CA 94608
Fun reading for the serious tech-head. Correspondents from the
various recording studios send in information about who is doing
what, where; a very strong source for networking information.

Music City News
50 Music Square W., Suite 601
P.O. Box 29275
Nashville, TN 37203

Music Connection Magazine
6640 Sunset Blvd., #120
Hollywood, CA 90028
This L.A.-based biweekly covers the Los Angeles scene like nothing else. Informative interviews with key A&R personnel and publishers. Very hip and not afraid to take chances. A must-have for
anyone living, hoping to live, or submitting material or acts to the
industry based in Los Angeles. Very inside information only available here. Highly recommended for serious professionals.

Music Week
Greater London House
Hampstead Rd.
London, NW1 7QZ
England

Musician
1515 Broadway, 39th Floor
New York, NY 10036
A Billboard publications magazine. Very hip inside stuff, interviews
with key players and bands. *Musician* also publishes a guide for
touring bands with information about the major cities, including a

comprehensive listing of clubs, who to contact, what type of music they book and other information.

Performance Magazine
1203 Lake St., Suite 200
Fort Worth, TX 76102
A weekly magazine for the touring business with valuable information on who is performing where, and grosses earned from the shows. They also have a yearly listing of management companies and agencies and other special issues throughout the year, including their Personal Manager guide in contacting talent.

Pollstar
4838 N. Blackstone Ave., 2nd Floor
Fresno, CA 93726
Also for the touring biz.

Radio and Records
1930 Century Park W.
Los Angeles, CA 90067
Just what the title says, this is the magazine that shows the progress of records via airplay. Highly recommended; cold, hard facts and statistics.

Recording Engineer/Producer
9221 Quivira Rd.
P.O. Box 12960
Overland Park, KS 66215

Recording Industry Sourcebook
3301 Barham Blvd., #300
Los Angeles, CA 90068
Published yearly, this is a magazine that has seen phenomenal growth. A copy sits on my desk at all times because it includes listings for record companies, managers, agents, lawyers, recording studios, producers, and virtually every other contact anyone could conceivably need in their career; highly recommended.

Record Week
216 Carlton
Toronto, Ontario, Canada

Rock and Soul
441 Lexington Ave.
New York, NY 10017

Rolling Stone
745 5th Ave.
New York, NY 10151
Movie, fashion, political magazine with music. I'm old enough to remember it as an underground music magazine in the late 1960s; my, how we've all changed. The *Stone* is still good at charting new music, trends and exposing new records.

RPM Weekly
6 Brentcliffe Rd.
Toronto, Ontario, Canada M4G 3Y2

Songtalk
% NAS
6381 Hollywood Blvd., Suite 780
Hollywood, CA 90028
Published quarterly, Paul Zollo's interviews with hit writers are always a joy to read; he's been able to access Bob Dylan, Paul Simon and Madonna. *Songtalk* is full of other good features, too, with a decided emphasis on material of interest to songwriters.

Songwriters Musepaper
P.O. Box 93759
Hollywood, CA 90093
The most widely read songwriter publication in North America with interviews, information, musical chairs (who is where in the business) and other articles on the craft and business of songwriting. Members of the Los Angeles Songwriters Showcase receive this magazine as a part of their membership. It is also available by subscription, and at "drop sites," music stores, studios, etc., in the Los Angeles area. This is a good place to begin to learn the names behind the hits; the *Songwriters Musepaper* uncovers information that you would not find elsewhere.

Spin
6 W. 18th St.
New York, NY 10011

Bob Guccionne Jr.'s entry into the rock world. Very hip and fun reading. It's like *Rolling Stone* used to be.

Variety
475 Park Ave. S., 2nd Floor
New York, NY 10016
Weekly film and television journal. *Variety* is a good source for finding movies that are in early stages of production and who is supervising the music for possible submissions.

Yellow Pages of Rock
Album Network
120 N. Victory Blvd., 3rd Floor
Burbank, CA 91502
Information about record distribution, radio stations and comprehensive listings of independent and major labels. This yearly book is another one that sits on my desk at all times; I recommend it highly for your desk too. The information is very consistent and the format is reader-friendly with interesting graphics and great-looking ads.

INDEX